THE BOOK OF MOVIE LISTS

I1021469

THE BOOK
OF MOVIE LISTS

BY GABE ESSOE

Published in Association with
Stan Corwin Productions

ARLINGTON HOUSE

Westport, Connecticut

THIS BOOK AND ITS COMPANION VOLUME ARE DEDICATED to my loving wife, Kelley, who is the most incredible woman I have ever known. She is my safe port in stormy weather, my shade in the heat of day, my glimmer of light when in darkness I have lost my way. I love her for who she is, for the support and love she gives me, and for the two beautiful, wonderful children we have made together—Joshua and Jordan—for they are, at the very least, an improvement on mankind.

Copyright © 1981 by Gabe Essoe.

All rights reserved. No part of this book may be reproduced in any form or by any electronic or mechanical means including information storage and retrieval systems without permission in writing from the publisher, except by a reviewer who may quote brief passages in a review.

"Rona Barrett's List of 17 Box Office Bombs of 1979," Copyright © 1980 by the Laufer Company. Reprinted by permission;

"A Baker's Dozen Most Often Broadcast Movies on TV," Copyright © 1977 by TV Guide. Reprinted by permission.

Arlington House/Publishers,
333 Post Road West,
Westport, Connecticut 06880.

Library of Congress Cataloging in Publication Data

Essoe, Gabe.
   The official book of movie lists.

   1. Moving-pictures—Miscellanea.   I. Title.
PN1998.E85   791.43   80-28178
ISBN 0-87000-496-4

Printed in the United States of America

Designed by Verne Bowman

9 8 7 6 5 4 3 2 1

ISBN 0-87000-520-0

CONTENTS

FOREWORD

The epitome in acting is to hit the big time, and the big time has always meant to make it in the movies. I started out doing radio, a lot of theatre, and I did a lot of work on television, both live and on film; but my goal was always to reach the heights in the motion picture business. *That* meant success.

My first experience with the movies came in 1950. At the time I was doing some live TV and just finishing a play with Helen Hayes, called *Mrs. McThing*. I had heard that they were going to be shooting a picture in New Hampshire and went up there from New York to see if I could get some work. I met a man who spoke with an accent, and after looking me over, he said: "You got good face, you come tomorrow and I give you screen test." I left there on cloud nine, full of the old P&V because I knew I was on my way in the movies, even though I knew it was only as an extra.

The next day, I showed up at the restaurant on Fifty-seventh Street, where I was told to go, and I had to push my way in through some 300 people. They were all getting the same screen test. I felt real downhearted, my hopes dashed to the ground. But then, that man I'd met in New Hampshire came over to me and told me to go away for a couple of hours, and then he'd give me the screen test. So I left, walking down Fifth Avenue. I had a dime in my pocket and had nowhere to go. Where can you even sit down on Fifth Avenue?

Sincerely
Ernest
Borgnine

In those days, they didn't even have bus benches on the street. And as I'm walking, I find myself at St. Patrick's Cathedral. Now, I'm not much of a praying man—I'm a real lousy Catholic—but I went in and got down on my knees. "Please, God," I said, "I need the work, you know."

When I went back, there were only a couple of people left and I was the last one to get tested. The man with the accent called me over and told me to sit on the stool, look camera right, then camera left, and say just one word. That was all there was to it, so I said: "Yessir." And he said, "Okay, roll it." And I said: "But, sir, what do you want me to say?" And he replied: "Just say the word *shit.* " I looked at him in amazement. *"Shit?"* And he said: "When you say that word, it makes you smile. You got a good smile, so just say it." So I did. I looked camera right, then camera left, and then said *shit.*

I got the job. It was only supposed to be three days work as an extra, but somehow I ended up with a featured part in my very first picture, *The Whistle at Eton Falls* (1951). It starred Dorothy Gish and Lloyd Bridges, and was directed by Robert Siodmak, that wonderful man with an accent who gave me that first test.

I hadn't always wanted to be an actor. I became one almost by accident. Following World War II, I was unemployed and casting about looking for a job. I was twenty-eight years old, had just finished ten years in the Navy, and was considering going back in for another ten to get a pension. My mother, God bless her, said to me out of the blue one day: "Why don't you try acting? You always did like to make a fool of yourself." It was as if a light had been lit in the darkness for me, and I suddenly knew that that was what I wanted.

My first Hollywood screen test was given to me by Max Arnow, casting director for Columbia studios at the time. He was looking for new faces in New York, and I managed to get a test, and somehow got to be last again. During the test, which was for a picture called *The Mob,* I was talking to an imaginary person, who was supposed to be Brod Crawford. Halfway through the scene, I backhanded him. When it was over, Max asked me why I had done that. I said: "I just felt the scene needed it." He nodded thoughtfully and said: "I'll see you in Hollywood." Well, by that time, I'd been through the mill and took it with a grain of salt. But true to his word, I ended up in Hollywood, in *The Mob* (1951), and with a better part than I had tested for. Charles Bronson was in it, too, just starting out like me.

A couple of years later, Max remembered me when they were casting *From Here to Eternity.* He kept pushing my name. And they'd

Movie and TV superstar Ernest Borgnine. He proved his star quality by winning an Academy Award for his portrayal of *Marty* in 1955.

say, "Who the hell is he?" They'd already cast somebody else, but MGM wouldn't release him right then, and they wanted to start right away. So Arnow brought me out to test for the part of Fatso Judson. I stuck out my gut and let it all hang out. And I got the part! I had dreamt about this two years before when I read the book. I told my wife then, "If anybody's going to play this part, I am." And sure enough, I ended up with it. It's amazing, but funny things do happen.

I remember a bit in Louella Parson's column soon after: ERNEST BORGNINE AS MARTY? It was there in big headlines, after I had tested for the part and all. Spencer Tracy came up to me and said: "Don't worry about her, kid, you're gonna be a star." And I said: "I don't know about that." And he said: "Well, I do. But just remember one thing. Always be nice on the way up, because then they'll be nice to you on the way down." I've never forgotten that.

The following year, he was up for the Academy Award for *Bad Day at Black Rock* (1955), which I had done with him. And I was up against him for *Marty*. And I won. To think that he had predicted it, and I had come out a star, even beat him at his own game. I was so thrilled, I can't tell you. How lucky can a guy be?

Well, we've come a long way from those days and the wonderful films we made then. Today, it seems that much of the glamour and the imagination is gone from the picture business. Films don't leave anything to the imagination anymore. Everything is too graphic and too explicit. And because of it, movies aren't as provocative or as entertaining anymore.

What was so captivating about films was that you could spend a few hours in a different world, a world that was more glamorous and more fun than our everyday lives. You could escape into a fantasy and not think about your troubles for a little while.

I love the movies. They're my life. I just wish we could make them like we used to. I miss the glamour, the excitement, the pizzazz, the tinsel. If we could lessen the emphasis on the almighty dollar, and put the emphasis back on entertainment, we'd all be in better shape. And, you know, we'd do much better at the box office than we're doing now.

ERNEST BORGNINE

PREFACE

The things that seem to most profoundly influence us for life are those that touch us deeply in our formative years. My formative years (though I sometimes feel that I'm still in them) were spent in a small Illinois town called Danville, which in boyhood memory looms much more expansive than it appeared to me when I visited there as an adult. It was hard to believe that the town had changed so much. But, of course, the town was still fairly much the same, and *I* had changed.

One of the first places I went to see was the Rivoli Theatre, just across the town square from Bolay's Hobbies where I used to gorge myself on second-hand comic books for a nickel apiece. Bolay's was still there, but the Rivoli, like the movie house in *The Last Picture Show,* had closed its doors and vanished, carrying with it a legion of memories and sensations. It saddened me, for it was at the Rivoli that I discovered movies in 1952.

The Rivoli. The name is still emotion-charged even after all these years. It was a world apart from everything else, where a young boy's imagination was totally enchanted. The very darkness inside seemed to shut out the existence of the lobby and beyond, and the only reality was what was going on up on the screen (in the days when it truly was silver). The collective excitement and enthusiasm within the darkened theatre was electric.

For a quarter apiece, my brothers and I could spend Saturday afternoon with Tim Holt and Rocky Lane in a double feature, along with a Bugs Bunny cartoon and a chapter from a *Blackhawk* serial. It was always a disappointment to me when the show ended, and I didn't know how I would make it through the week ahead until I could return to find out if Blackhawk escaped from the burning building in the next serial chapter. Of course he did, and there were two new features on the bill. Over the score of months that we made our weekly trek, we grew to know and love Roy Rogers, Gene Autry, Rex Allen, Lash LaRue, Buster Crabbe, Rod Cameron, Hopalong Cassidy, Abbott and Costello, the Bowery Boys, Francis the talking mule, and Charlie Chan, among others.

Apart from the B-Westerns (which forever changed me at heart from sodbuster to cowpoke), my favorite films were the *Tarzans*. They captured me completely. Johnny Weissmuller. Lex Barker. Now, *there* were heroes! The first movie to make an indelible mark on my budding psyche was *Tarzan the Ape Man* (1932), which ran with *Tarzan Escapes* (1936). With those two pictures, there began an unyielding Walter Mitty desire in me to be king of the jungle, which I finally dealt with sixteen years later by writing a book, *Tarzan of the Movies*. So, I guess you could say that Tarzan has been a positive influence.

Like the millions of kids who earned their spurs in theatres like the Rivoli, I have been a lifelong film buff. This book is a testimony to the endless hours of enjoyment and fantasy fulfillment given to me by the movies, and also an affectionate nod to all the men and women who have made the movies what they are today.

ACKNOWLEDGMENTS:
The Helping Hands

On a project like this, the workload was much more immense than meets the eye. The number of people involved was staggering. A computer would have been extremely helpful in keeping all of the diverse elements quasi-organized: the hundreds of addresses, phone numbers, the photos, the tons of reference books and magazines—not to mention the wads of notes and random scribblings that occurred whenever unpredictable inspiration struck (most often while driving, or in the middle of the night, or in restaurants, or in the bathroom). My office looked like the White House document-shredding station for six months—and in fact still does.

My sanity was preserved only through the help and support of scores of absolutely wonderful people who gave of their time and energies freely and generously. Trying to acknowledge them all adequately on this page is a bit like trying to pass an elephant through the eye of a needle. However, I want to publicly state that without their assistance, the book you hold in your hands would not have been possible. I'm indebted to: my wife, Kelley, for her creative input and unflagging encouragement; my close friend and mentor, Doug Benton, for his guidance and advice; Stan Corwin, for his patience and inspiration; my agent and confidante, Beverly Iser, for opening a lot of doors; Ernest Borgnine, for his friendship and participation; dear friend John LeBold, curator of the Hollywood Museum, for pictures and research; Michael Levine and TV News, for photos and research; Robert Osborne, for a herculean effort and photos; Clint Eastwood, for the first lists; Charles Champlin, *Los Angeles Times,* for his friendship and enthusiasm; George Kennedy; Vera Miles; Dennis Weaver; John Ritter; Jim Ashton; Jim

Murray, *Los Angeles Times;* John Michaeli, Hanna-Barbera, Inc.; Paul Novak; Mae West; Eileen Ford; Erica Jong; Suzy Mallery; Richard Lamparski; Robert Stack; Johnny Weissmuller; Jock Mahoney; Keith Larsen; Rex Allen; Dr. Laurence J. Peter; Mr. Blackwell; Bob Michaelson; Burt Reynolds; Nancy Streebeck; Mario Andretti; Kay Gable; Lou Ferrigno; Buddy Ebsen, for his friendship and help; Dick Martin; Fred MacMurray; Debbie Reynolds; David Rose; Anton La Vey; Bob Munden; Lash LaRue; Forrest J. Ackerman; Esme Chandlee; Dina Merrill; Mel Blanc; Charlton Heston; Harvey Perry; Melvin Belli; Shirley Jones; Newell Emmons; my IBM Selectric II, which suffered a lot of abuse without once throwing a temper tantrum; and Shelly Weinstock, for expertly copy-editing everything.

THE BOOK OF MOVIE LISTS

Vivien Leigh and Clark Gable in *Gone With the Wind* (1939), the most popular movie of all time.

1 CHAPTER

CRITIC'S CHOICE

Or: *Some Bests, Some Worsts . . . and How You Can't Please Everybody*

THE 10 GREATEST AMERICAN FILMS OF ALL TIME

To celebrate its 10th Anniversary, the American Film Institute in 1977 conducted the largest survey in the history of film studies. A poll questionnaire was sent to 35,000 members across the nation and around the world to select the ultimate ten best American films of all time.

1. GONE WITH THE WIND (1939)
   Clark Gable, Vivien Leigh; directed by Victor Fleming
2. CITIZEN KANE (1941)
   Produced, directed, and co-written by Orson Welles
3. CASABLANCA (1942)
   Humphrey Bogart, Ingrid Bergman; directed by Michael Curtiz
4. THE AFRICAN QUEEN (1952)
   Humphrey Bogart, Katharine Hepburn; directed by John Huston
5. THE GRAPES OF WRATH (1940)
   Henry Fonda, Jane Darwell; directed by John Ford
6. ONE FLEW OVER THE CUCKOO'S NEST (1975)
   Jack Nicholson, Louise Fletcher; directed by Milos Forman
7. SINGIN' IN THE RAIN (1952)
   Gene Kelly, Debbie Reynolds; directed by Gene Kelly and Stanley Donen

Hans Solo (Harrison Ford) and Chewbacca lazer blasted their way to the highest grosses ever in *Star Wars*.

8. STAR WARS (1977)
   Mark Hamill, Carrie Fisher, Harrison Ford; written and directed by George Lucas
9. 2001: A SPACE ODYSSEY (1968)
   Keir Dullea, Gary Lockwood; directed by Stanley Kubrick
10. THE WIZARD OF OZ (1939)
   Judy Garland, Frank Morgan, Bert Lahr, Jack Haley, Ray Bolger; directed by Victor Fleming

CHARLES CHAMPLIN'S 16 ALL-TIME BEST FILMS

The Arts Editor of the *Los Angeles Times,* Charles Champlin, is the foremost film critic on the West Coast, and perhaps in the country.

Says Champlin: "I hate lists because they're either a joke or a year's research. In speaking of the all-time best films ever made, for example, do we include, by reputation only, the Senegalese film, *Mbu-Mbu, Boy of the Village,* which was declared a classic by the 200 people who saw it before it was eaten by army ants?

"I would hedge about with the usual caveats that an all-time best film in 1915 is not necessarily the same as an all-time ditto in 1980;

The Wizard of Oz (1939), with Jack Haley as the Tinman, Judy Garland as Dorothy, Ray Bolger as the Scarecrow, and Bert Lahr as the Cowardly Lion, was voted the tenth most popular film of all time.

there has to be a monumental allowance for having gotten there first, and thus established part of the language of film. So that, racist as we may think it now, you couldn't not include *Birth of a Nation*. Silly as it plays now, you couldn't not include *Cabinet of Dr. Caligari*, or Murnau's *The Last Laugh*, or Eisenstein's *Potemkin*, or Hitchcock's *The Lodger*, or Ford's *The Iron Horse*, which I remember from a single viewing forty years ago; or Ford's *The Grapes of Wrath*, or Renoir's *Grand Illusion*, or the collective *Casablanca*, or *Top Hat* and *Singin' in the Rain* as definitive musicals, or Bergman's *Cries and Whispers* for taking the film as deep into the soul as it has ever gone. *Citizen Kane*, of course, for technique and humanity, both. I might finally add *Midnight Cowboy* and *Last Tango in Paris*, and define each as a film after which other films would not be done quite the same again."

Thus, chronologically, and with directors:

1. *BIRTH OF A NATION* (1915), David Wark Griffith
2. *CABINET OF DR. CALIGARI* (1919), Robert Weine
3. *THE LAST LAUGH* (1924), F. W. Murnau
4. *THE IRON HORSE* (1924), John Ford
5. *POTEMKIN* (1925), Sergei Eisenstein
6. *THE LODGER* (1926), Alfred Hitchcock
7. *THE CROWD* (1928), King Vidor
8. *TOP HAT* (1935), Mark Sandrich
9. *GRAND ILLUSION* (1937), Jean Renoir
10. *GRAPES OF WRATH* (1940), John Ford
11. *CITIZEN KANE* (1941), Orson Welles
12. *CASABLANCA* (1942), Michael Curtiz
13. *SINGIN' IN THE RAIN* (1952), Gene Kelly and Stanley Donen
14. *MIDNIGHT COWBOY* (1969), John Schlesinger
15. *CRIES AND WHISPERS* (1972), Ingmar Bergman
16. *LAST TANGO IN PARIS* (1972), Bernardo Bertolucci

CHARLES CHAMPLIN'S TOP 10 DIRECTORS OF SUSPENSE

1. ALFRED HITCHCOCK
2. ALFRED HITCHCOCK
3. ALFRED HITCHCOCK
4. ALFRED HITCHCOCK
5. ALFRED HITCHCOCK
6. ALFRED HITCHCOCK
7. ALFRED HITCHCOCK
8. ALFRED HITCHCOCK
9. ALFRED HITCHCOCK
10. ALFRED HITCHCOCK

"Hitchcock was the only true master of suspense. There are others who keep you in a kind of suspense, wondering exactly how much

Orson Welles in the title role of *Citizen Kane* (1941), a motion picture classic. He also directed and coauthored the screenplay with Herman J. Mankiewicz.

butchery they're going to dump in your lap, but no one has yet rivaled Hitch for putting the innocent in jeopardy and making you care if he or she or they will get out of it.''

CHARLES CHAMPLIN'S LIST OF 3 HIGHLY DISAPPOINTING FILM ADAPTATIONS OF HIGHLY TREASURED LITERARY PROPERTIES

Champlin: "The thing about disappointments, as about bad pictures generally, is that some kind and sparing mental process ushers them out of mind before they can pollute the surrounding cells. There are, however, some that stick like tar to new tennis shoes. And these are three literary properties that I treasured and hated to see done so unsatisfactorily.''

1. THE GREAT GATSBY (1974)
   Robert Redford, Mia Farrow, Bruce Dern, Karen Black. Directed by Jack Clayton. Based on F. Scott Fitzgerald's book of the same name. Script by Francis Ford Coppola.
2. THEY SHOOT HORSES, DON'T THEY? (1969)
   Jane Fonda, Michael Sarrazin, Gig Young, Susannah York, Red Buttons. D: Sidney Pollack. Based on the novel by Horace McCoy.
3. THE LAST TYCOON (1976)
   Robert De Niro, Tony Curtis, Robert Mitchum, Jeanne Moreau, Jack Nicholson. D: Elia Kazan. Harold Pinter adaptation of the F. Scott Fitzgerald novel.

CHARLES CHAMPLIN'S 8 MEMORABLE ONE-LINER REVIEWS

"One of my favorites is from Vincent Canby":

1. "Watching *Song of Norway* (1970) is like being trapped in an aerial tramway with nothing to read.''

   ". . . and a few of my own":
2. "*1776* (1972) is as American as the turkey, which it closely resembles.''
3. "The cobra in *Death on the Nile* (1978) at least has a plot to hiss in.''
4. "The simple secret of *Lucky Lady*'s (1975) plot is that if at first you don't ménage, trois, trois again.''
5. "There will be few complaints that *The Hunter* (1980) is only ninety-seven minutes long; enough is enough.''
6. "The mistake in *Raise the Titanic* (1980) was keeping her afloat long after the picture had begun to sink.''

7. "Robert Altman's *Health* (1980) has easily won this year's Listerine Prize for lousy word of mouth."
8. "*Private Benjamin* (1980) is a movie you don't salute, you court-martial; the script went AWOL."

RONA BARRETT'S LIST OF 17 BOX OFFICE BOMBS OF 1979

If any single personality can be said to fully capture the evolving essence of the New Hollywood, both in print and on television, it is Rona Barrett. Her success is due not only to her sense of showmanship, which is highly polished, but also to her unique reportorial style which combines a hard-hitting newsroom approach with the glamour vernacular of the traditional Hollywood gossip columnist. Today's film scene is dominated by Miss Rona in ways far more sophisticated than Louella Parsons or Hedda Hopper ever dreamed possible.

Miss Rona (writing in *Rona Barrett Looks at the Oscars*) says: "What better way to end a decade than with a big bang? Well, that depends on which side of the cash register you're standing. Here's a list of movies that we all waited for when we might've had more fun eating the popcorn at home. . . ."

1. 1941
   Proof positive that a talented director like Steven Spielberg *(Jaws, Close Encounters)* can take almost $40 million of Universal's money and come up with a multistarred "comedy" with absolutely no laughs . . . managed to be racist, sophomoric, and trite all at once.
2. METEOR
   How could director Ronald Neame spend almost $17 million . . . and then the best "special effect" is Sean Connery's toupée?
3. AIRPORT 1979: THE CONCORDE
   Well, this trash is to movies what airline food is to gourmet meals. . . . Shame on Universal for spending over $10 million on this . . . and then never answering the question: Just what in the hell was John Davidson doing in the jacuzzi ·with Andrea Marcovicci?
4. PLAYERS
   A multimillion-dollar tennis movie—that didn't score. . . . Maybe it was just the fact that (1) Ali MacGraw can't act, (2) Dean-Paul Martin can't act, or (3) nobody really gives a fig about Ali MacGraw. . . .
5. HANOVER STREET
   Costar Harrison Ford, as Lesley Anne-Down's GI lover, gets our Ryan O'Neal Underacting Award for '79 . . . and '80 . . . and '81.

6. BEYOND THE POSEIDON ADVENTURE

Producer-Director Irwin Allen got performances out of a star-studded cast that found Sally Field and Michael Caine so damned wooden they could have floated the *Poseidon* up to the surface in ten seconds flat.

7. THE PROPHECY

At last—yet another entry in the seemingly never-ending Talia Shire Film Festival of Bad, Bad Movies. . . . The only horrifying thing about this dud was—you guessed it—watching Talia Shire overact.

8. GOLDEN GIRL

Susan Anton, TV's Muriel Cigar Girl, was unusually cast as an Olympic runner. . . . well, hate to steal a line from the likes of Stanley Kramer, but the runner stumbles.

9. SUNBURN

The only thing tinier than the bikini Farrah Fawcett wore in this comedy-thriller was La Farrah's talent.

10. QUINTET

Ever wonder what Paul Newman would look like in a flop? This Robert Altman dud showed you. . . .

11. SCAVENGER HUNT

You thought Dirk Benedict had problems in TV's "Battlestar Galactica?" In *Scavenger Hunt,* he really had problems—in one mercifully brief scene, he was out-acted by a jock strap.

12. NIGHTWING

It will make you fwow up.

13. SKATETOWN U.S.A.

We can imagine only one thing worse than having to sit through this movie one more time: a Leif Garret concert.

14. DREAMER

We wouldn't dream of saying something so obvious about a bowling movie as: It belongs in the gutter. But we'll go ahead anyway and say it (there, we feel better already) . . .

15. THE RUNNER STUMBLES

A "religious melodrama" with Dick Van Dyke as a priest (Dick Van Dyke as a priest?!? Wait—it gets better/worse—choose one) who falls in love with young nun Kathleen Quinlan. So stupefying as to give sincerity a bad name.

16. LUNA

The scene where Jill Clayburgh literally masturbates her son, played by Matthew Barry, is one of the most unpleasant in cinema history. . . . Why does Hollywood finance such junk? For art's sake? Sure . . .

17. CUBA

United Artists' very own Bay of Pigs, thanks to Richard Lester's hapless direction, Charles Woods' flaccid script, and Sean Connery's and Brooke Adams' charisma-minus acting.

JIM MURRAY'S LIST OF THE 8 BEST HOLLYWOOD SPORTS MOVIES

The kingpin of the *Los Angeles Times* Sports Section is Jim Murray, who has been named Sportswriter of the Year fourteen of the last seventeen years by his colleagues in the National Association of Sportscasters and Sportswriters. In 1961, eighteen years out of Trinity College in his native Hartford, Connecticut, Murray started with the *Times*. En route, he had covered politics and films for *Time* Magazine, and helped launch *Sports Illustrated.* He hadn't really intended to become a sportswriter: "Sometimes I think it would be better to be a failed playwright. In football, for example, I can't for the life of me understand why it's so hard to complete a pass. The ball's so god-damned big, and the guy's standing maybe eight yards away some-times. It mystifies me. I suppose it's because there're people coming at you . . ."

1. PRIDE OF THE YANKEES (1942)
   Director: Sam Wood; Gary Cooper, Teresa Wright, Babe Ruth, Walter

Former baseball superstar Babe Ruth, with Gary Cooper as Lou Gehrig in *Pride of the Yankees* (1942).

Brennan, Dan Duryea. "There wasn't too much sports in it, though it was the biography of Lou Gehrig, but it was a damn good film."

2. REQUIEM FOR A HEAVYWEIGHT (1962)
   D: Ralph Nelson; Anthony Quinn, Jackie Gleason, Mickey Rooney, Julie Harris, Muhammad Ali. Based on Rod Serling's great teleplay. "There's a scene with Tony Quinn and Jackie Gleason that I'll never forget."

3. CHAMPION (1949)
   D: Mark Robson; Kirk Douglas, Marilyn Maxwell, Arthur Kennedy, Ruth Roman.

4. BRIAN'S SONG (1970)
   D: Buzz Kulik; Billy Dee Williams, James Caan, Jack Warden, Shelly Fabares. "This was a real emotional, gripping picture."

5. THE GREAT WHITE HOPE (1970)
   D: Martin Ritt; James Earl Jones, Jane Alexander. Story of famed heavyweight champion, Jack Jefferson.

6. FEAR STRIKES OUT (1957)
   D: Robert Mulligan; Anthony Perkins, Karl Malden, Norma Moore. "Perkins is good as Piersall."

7. NAVY BLUE AND GOLD (1937)
   D: Sam Wood; Robert Young, James Stewart, Lionel Barrymore, Billie Burke. "It's sorta hackneyed, but entertaining, and I loved it when I was a kid."

8. KNUTE ROCKNE, ALL AMERICAN (1940)
   D: Lloyd Bacon; Pat O'Brien, Gale Page, Donald Crisp, and Ronald Reagan as star player George "Gipper" Gipp.

JIM MURRAY'S LIST OF 8 SPORTS MOVIES THAT FAILED TO SCORE

1. SPIRIT OF WEST POINT (1947)
   "This was with Glen Davis and Tom Harmon, both pals of mine, but the movie was terrible. Certainly not one of the best."

2. THE LONGEST YARD (1974)
   "I hated it. I like Burt Reynolds very much, but I thought the picture was overrated."

3. HEAVEN CAN WAIT (1978)
   "I hate fantasy. I saw and liked the original, when he wasn't a football player."

4. ANGELS IN THE OUTFIELD (1951)
   "Ohgodno. When you say fantasy or spoof, you lose me. I just can't relate to it."

5. ROCKY (1976)
   "A lot of people liked it, but I wasn't enamored of it."

6. ONE ON ONE (1977)
   "I have never seen a basketball movie that was any good."
7. FOLLOW THE SUN (1951)
   "I revere Ben Hogan, the golfer whose life this was about, but this movie with Glenn Ford was terrible."
8. SOMEBODY UP THERE LIKES ME (1956)
   "Paul Newman as Rocky Graziano. Not one of my favorites."

HANNA AND BARBERA'S LIST OF THE 4 MOST OUTSTANDING ANIMATED FEATURES OF ALL TIME

William Hanna and Joe Barbera, though now identified with limited animation Saturday morning cartoon shows, were two of the pioneers of animation. The partners created and produced the seven-time Academy-Award-winning *Tom and Jerry* theatrical cartoons for Metro-Goldwyn-Mayer in the 1940s. And really know their cartoons.

1. Walt Disney's SNOW WHITE AND THE SEVEN DWARFS (1937)
   "This was not only the first animation *feature,* but it was the first production of real quality."
2. Walt Disney's FANTASIA (1940)
   "Wonderful incorporation of music and fantasy animation and animation techniques."
3. Walt Disney's PINOCCHIO (1939)
   "The best exhibition of animation art and direction."
4. Walt Disney's 101 DALMATIANS (1961)
   "This was the first use of Xerox process for the line art, helping to preserve the animators' true lines and subtleties."

CHARLES LABBE'S LIST OF THE 4 BEST FILMS DEPICTING ADOLPH HITLER

Charles worked his way up in the American Nazi Party to the rank of captain and is currently second in command of the National Socialist Movement, based in Cincinnati, Ohio.

1. OUR HITLER (West Germany, 1979)
   A monumental 8½-hour documentary done completely in German. Uses footage from such films as *Triumph of the Will.* Covers Nazi Germany completely from the Munich riots in 1923 to the fall of Berlin in 1945. There are scenes in concentration camps and more. It analyzes Hitler and delves into the effects of Wagner's anti-Semitism and Aryan attitudes on Hitler. There are also interviews and newsreels in this film. This is the best

study of Hitler and Nazism for the serious student. However, its sheer length will ward some people off.

2. THE LAST TEN DAYS OF HITLER (Germany, 1956)
A gripping, detailed depiction of the final days of Hitler, portrayed excellently by Oskar Werner.

3. HITLER: A CAREER (West Germany, 1979)
A very selective film in that its treatment of Hitler leaves out several facets of his life, such as his oppressive nature and the totalitarian society of the Nazis. It uses good film footage to focus on Hitler the orator and the man, and his ability to evoke an emotional following. The film tastefully omits mention of concentration camps. It screened with English subtitles.

4. HITLER (U.S., 1962)
Richard Basehart as Hitler in a cerebral portrayal. Traces his rise to power. Has good intentions, but has nothing unseen before and doesn't have the proper production values necessary for the scope of the real story.

... THE WORST FILM ABOUT HITLER

1. THEY SAVED HITLER'S BRAIN (1964)
Ludicrous tale about Hitler's decapitated head being kept alive by fanatics on a Caribbean Island.

... THE BEST COMEDY ABOUT HITLER

1. THE GREAT DICTATOR (1940)
Charlie Chaplin satirized Hitler, and Hitler was supposed to have seen the film and enjoyed it.

... THE 2 BEST FICTIONAL FILMS ABOUT POST–WORLD WAR II NAZIS

1. THE BOYS FROM BRAZIL (1978)
2. THE ODESSA FILE (1974)

... THE BEST FACTUAL FILM ABOUT POST–WORLD WAR II NAZIS

1. CALIFORNIA REICH (1977)
Documentary study of the National Socialist White Workers Party in California.

Charles Chaplin satirizes the histrionics of Adolph Hitler in *The Great Dictator* (1940).

THE FIRST ANNUAL "WASTE OF FILM" FESTIVAL FEATURING 10 ROBERT ALTMAN LOSERS

Director/producer Robert Altman is apparently distressed with what the movie industry has to offer these days. In a *Penthouse* magazine interview, he disclosed that he doesn't go to the movies anymore because "It's a waste of time. I'll hear about an interesting film, and I'll think, 'Oh, God, a good one managed to slip through.' " But the industry, he feels, is generally in terrible shape, and he's afraid it will become "just like Broadway, which has become a joke."

Altman has genuine reason to be distressed. He has become the sort of joke he fears for Hollywood. More than any other big name director, he consistently churns out films which are inane, vague, pretentious, unentertaining, and totally undisciplined. With perhaps only three exceptions—*M*A*S*H* (1970), *McCabe and Mrs. Miller* (1971), and *Nashville* (1975)—all of Altman's pictures have been as boring and superficial as they are experimental, and as meandering and pointless as they are individualistic. It is an endless source of wonder, after all of the turkeys he has unleashed on the paying public, that he manages to continue making films.

1. HEALTH (1980)
   After 20th Century-Fox saw the self-indulgent mess in which Altman had wasted the talents of James Garner, Glenda Jackson, Carol Burnett, and Lauren Bacall, the studio held up release for months, until finally releasing it at year's end to manfully use it as a tax loss. *Los Angeles Times* critic Charles Champlin, who champions Altman's originality, wrote: "Not for the first time Altman seems to have set out with an unjelled script (or perhaps this time, a jelled script that was later left in the Florida sun too long), hoping to find the movie once shooting began. But the movie art is still discipline as well as inspiration, and the basic problem with *Health* is that it never appears to know where the exit is, or how to get there."

2. QUINTET (1979)
   This senseless garbage made everyone's Ten Worst list. Rona Barrett wrote: "Did you wonder just what in hades those dogs in almost every other scene were chewing on? No, not the scenery—Paul Newman did that. Yes, it was . . . the script! Better an avalanche should have covered the silly thing before they went to the trouble of filming it."

3. A WEDDING (1978)
   A few amusing moments do not a picture make. Carol Burnett, Mia Farrow, Geraldine Chaplin, and other talents were lost in this uneven, unfocused look at family intrigues at a wedding.

4. THREE WOMEN (1977)
   Completely unconventional, and heavy going for anyone without a detailed program. Only the director knows for sure what's going on, and we're not even so sure about him.
5. WELCOME TO L.A. (1977)
   Though only produced by Altman, it undeniably bears his stamp and plays like a heavy-handed cynical injoke.
6. BUFFALO BILL AND THE INDIANS (1976)
   Altman makes the dull and belabored point that Buffalo Bill was a fraud; perhaps the film was more than just a little autobiographical.
7. CALIFORNIA SPLIT (1974)
   Rambling, muddled look at the emptiness of gambling which never makes a point; it proved to be just another futile exercise in excess.
8. THIEVES LIKE US (1973)
   If you like Midwestern scenery, atmosphere, and nice characterizations, this is for you; but stay away if you also like story, pace, and a film that gets someplace other than where it starts.
9. THE LONG GOODBYE (1972)
   Elliott Gould tries real hard but can't overcome the lack of direction; Altman stylized the detective genre right into a coma.
10. IMAGES (1972)
    In this ultra-weird outing, you're never sure whether you're watching Susannah York's craziness or Altman's craziness, or if this is the way he sees reality. And if it is indicative of Altman's special vision of life, then it explains why his films never quite touch down on ground.

2 CHAPTER

SOMEBODY UP THERE LIKES ME

Or: *Jeez! Lookit My Oscar!*

ROBERT OSBORNE'S LIST OF 11 OF OSCAR'S MOST EMBARRASSING MOMENTS

Robert Osborne, raconteur and wit, and columnist and critic for *The Hollywood Reporter,* has since 1978 been the official biographer of "Oscar." He was thus designated by the Academy of Motion Picture Arts and Sciences, not only because of his knowledge of the past-and-current film scene, but also because his 1965 book, *Academy Awards Illustrated,* had long been considered the definitive history of the annual Academy Awards. His official "biography," *50 Golden Years of Oscar,* went on to become a Literary Guild selection, a best-seller in its field and the recipient of two national book awards for excellence.

Osborne is also a lecturer; a frequent guest of network talk shows; has just completed a series of interviews on film sets for Dinah Shore's TV show; and is currently doing interviews with celebrities for Select-TV, a subscription television system.

Osborne states: "I don't really want it passed around that I am, in reality, a gypsy child, born in Poland and moved to Newfoundland at the age of puberty (six). I worked in the steel mills there until I saw my first film, a Tim Holt Western, and knew I had to become a Hollywood reporter. But since I've never been able to do Tim much good, I don't really want this phase publicized."

1. THE GEORGE C. SCOTT SNUB

   Scott was named Best Actor for 1970 (for *Patton*) but refused to accept the award because, in his opinion, "the contest is made more important than the achievement." Earlier, in 1961, he'd been nominated for Best Supporting Actor (for *The Hustler*) and similarly refused the nomination. (At least the guy's consistent.) His name was kept on the ballot nevertheless.

2. THE STREAKER

   While David Niven was on stage presenting an award in 1974, a thirty-three-year-old advertising man named Robert Opel—naked as the Oscar itself—suddenly bolted across the stage in full view of several million viewers. Ad-libbed Niven: "Just think. The only laugh that man will probably ever get is for stripping and showing his shortcomings."

3. THE CASE OF ROBERT RICH

   In 1956, the Oscar for Best Original Screenplay went to Robert Rich for *The Brave One*. But it soon became obvious that there was no such man. For years, Academy addicts speculated about who the real R. R. might be, and why the mystery? Nineteen years after the rhubarb, the truth came out. The real author was Dalton Trumbo, who'd used a pseudonym due to the political climate of the time; he'd been blacklisted during the Hollywood witch-hunts. Finally, however, he got his long-overdue Oscar.

4. THE GATE-CRASHER

   Despite precautions that rival White House security, and despite the 125 uniformed policemen on duty, a gate-crasher named Stan Berman managed to saunter on stage during the 1961 Oscar telecast, took over the podium, and presented a homemade replica of an Academy Award statuette to a bewildered Bob Hope.

5. FRANK CAPRA'S "LONG WALK"

   In announcing the Best Director Award for 1932–'33, Oscar Master-of-Ceremonies Will Rogers drawled on about "my good friend, Frank." Nominee Frank Capra was halfway to the stage when Rogers added, "That's Frank *Lloyd* for *Cavalcade*," leaving Capra with egg on his face. He returned to his seat from what he later described as "the longest crawl in history."

6. THE BRANDO REJECTION

   When Marlon Brando won his first Oscar in 1954 for *On the Waterfront*, he showed up—in a tux, yet—to receive his statue and obligatory kisses from co-winners, like Grace Kelly. In 1972, however, when he won for *The Godfather*, he refused the award and sent a young Indian girl named Sacheen Littlefeather (later identified as an actress named Maria

Cruz) to read his reasons: He objected to the industry's treatment of Indians in films, on TV, and in movie reruns.

7. THE YOUNG AMERICANS (AND THE RETURNED OSCAR)

In 1968, a documentary called *The Young Americans* won an Oscar—but a few weeks later it had to be given back. It was discovered that the film had been shown in a theatre in the preceding calendar year (1967) and was therefore ineligible for a 1968 award. It's the first and only time an Oscar had to be recalled.

8. THE CHILL WILLS PLUG FOR VOTES

Longtime character actor Chill Wills received his first Oscar nomination in 1960, as Best Supporting Actor for *The Alamo.* With a little too much help from legendary publicist Russell Birdwell, he went on a campaign for votes that some feel ultimately killed his chances of winning. The campaign got so blatant at one point that Wills took out an ad saying: "All my *Alamo* buddies are praying for me to win harder than the real Alamo fighters prayed for their lives." Which brought a terse reply from one of the *Alamo* buddies, John Wayne. And Groucho Marx got the last word with a trade ad saying: "Dear Chill, I'm voting for Sal Mineo."

9. THE MIXED-UP ENGRAVER

After Spencer Tracy won his 1937 Oscar for *Captains Courageous,* the statue itself was later sent out to be inscribed, but came back, much to the Academy's embarrassment, engraved: "To Dick Tracy."

10. THE RED-FACED FINALE

The worst end to an Oscar telecast came in 1958, when Jerry Lewis shared emcee chores with several other stars, including Bob Hope and Laurence Olivier. The final award had been presented, and ninety stars were amassed on stage to say "goodnight," when someone looked at the clock and discovered they still had twenty minutes of showtime to fill. Lewis tried, in vain, to save the situation by grabbing a baton, conducting the orchestra, clowning, and ordering the self-conscious and confused onstage celebrities (like John Wayne, Sophia Loren, Bette Davis, Gary Cooper) to dance. It didn't work. NBC finally pulled the plug and filled the time gap with a sports review.

11. THE BIGGEST UPSET OF THEM ALL

So sure was everyone in 1947 that Rosalind Russell would win the Best Actress Award for *Mourning Becomes Electra,* that it was considered a "no contest" ballot. A giant post-award victory party was planned in her honor. When presenter Fredric March tore open the envelope to announce the winner's name, Russell was halfway out of her seat, adjusting her dress, ready to walk down the aisle to collect her prize. But the name he read—totally unexpected—was Loretta Young, considered the least likely of all of the five nominees. She obviously had not expected to win because the dress she wore was a huge emerald-green taffeta that clearly hadn't been designed for climbing stairs to a stage.

arlon Brando in the role of Vito Coreleone in *The Godfather* (1972), for which
: won, but refused to accept, the Academy Award.

3 LEGENDS OF HOW OSCAR GOT HIS NAME

The Academy of Motion Picture Arts and Sciences was born in the afterdinner conversation at Louis B. Mayer's beach house in early 1927, during which the then-powerful studio chief of Metro-Goldwyn-Mayer exclaimed that he had "a wonderful idea for an organization to represent the entire industry as a whole."

The idea caught on and two months later, Articles of Incorporation were presented, and the first officers were elected: Douglas Fairbanks (president), M. C. Levee (treasurer), and Frank Woods (secretary).

The following year, an Award of Merit was proposed to recognize excellence in a dozen or so categories, to be presented in a gala annual event, as much for public relations as for internal acknowledgment. MGM art director Cedric Gibbons designed the now-familiar statuette, and sculptor George Stanley was paid $500 to cast the first figure. It was 13½ inches high, weighing 8¾ pounds; it was made of gold-plated Brittania metal.

Sometime during the first decade of its life, the nickname of "Oscar" was tagged to the Academy Award, and, at various times, three people have been credited with the christening:

1. The official version is that in 1931, MARGARET HERRICK, a long-time executive director of the Academy, but then a newly hired librarian, observed at the sight of the statuette: "Why, it looks like my uncle, Oscar." Other employees of the Academy took up the nickname and its use began to spread.
2. Hollywood columnist SIDNEY SKOLSKY says he made up the name Oscar because he got tired of referring to the Academy Award as "the statuette."
3. BETTE DAVIS, who won her first Oscar in 1935 (for *Dangerous*) and is the only woman ever to be president of the Academy, insists that she dubbed it for her first husband, Harmon Oscar Nelson.

The first Academy Award Presentation ceremonies was witnessed by some 250 people at the Hollywood Roosevelt Hotel on May 16, 1929. Today, an estimated 300 million people watch the annual festivities on television.

ROBERT OSBORNE'S LIST OF THE 12 MOST MEMORABLE OSCAR ACCEPTANCE SPEECHES

1. LOUISE FLETCHER, 1975
   Winning the Best Actress Award for *One Flew Over the Cuckoo's Nest*,

Bette Davis, Marilyn Monroe, and George Sanders in the unforgettable *All About Eve* (1950), which won Oscars for Best Picture, Best Direction, Best Screenplay, and Best Supporting Actor (Sanders).

she gave her acceptance speech partially in sign language for her deaf parents watching at home on television in Birmingham, Alabama. "I want to say thank you . . . for teaching me to have a dream," she told them. "You are seeing my dream come true."

2. GREER GARSON, 1947

In accepting her award for *Mrs. Miniver,* Best Actress Garson gave what some declare is the longest acceptance speech in Oscar history. But, as legends often do, reports on the actual length have become exaggerated, like that famous report of Mark Twain's premature death. Some say the talkathon went on for over an hour; others insist it lasted no more than six minutes at most; but whatever the length, it's the most famous for duration.

3. DIMITRI TIOMKIN, 1954

In winning the award for music scoring for *The High and the Mighty,*

Tiomkin accepted his statue by thanking a few helpers by name: "Brahms, Bach, Beethoven, Richard Strauss, Johann Strauss . . ."

4. INGRID BERGMAN, 1974

   When she received her third Academy Award (for Best Supporting Actress in *Murder on the Orient Express*), she devoted her "thank you" speech to extolling the talents of another nominee, Valentina Cortesa. "Forgive me, Valentina," she summed up, "I didn't mean to win . . ."

5. VANESSA REDGRAVE, 1977

   Redgrave got into some hot water—as others have done on occasion— by using her Oscar win as a platform to air some political views, specifically in critical references to "militant Zionist hoodlums" who protested her personal political beliefs and actions on (nonacting, non-Oscar) matters.

6. RUTH GORDON, 1968

   After a lifetime in the theatre as an actress and playwright, Gordon at age seventy-two won her first Oscar as a performer for Best Supporting Actress in *Rosemary's Baby*. She noted dryly, "I can't tell ya how encouragin' a thing like this is . . ."

7. JAMES STEWART, 1960

   Stewart, in accepting a Special Oscar for pal Gary Cooper, momentarily broke into tears, cueing a worldwide audience to learn what only a few close friends were aware of: that Cooper was dying of cancer.

8. FREDRIC MARCH, 1931–32

   Tying with actor Wallace Beery for the Best Actor Award, March accepted his prize (for *Dr. Jekyll and Mr. Hyde*) with a definite flair. By a strange coincidence, both actors had adopted children just shortly before winning their awards, prompting March to note: "Under the circumstances, it seems a little off that Wally and I were both given awards for the best male performance of the year . . ."

9. EVA MARIE SAINT, 1954

   Extremely pregnant the night she received her Best Actress Award for *On the Waterfront,* Saint tried to contain her excitement but couldn't. Breaking into an emotion-charged laugh, she said: "I think . . . I may have the baby . . . right here!"

10. KATHARINE HEPBURN, 1974

    Making her first appearance at the annual Academy Award ceremonies, despite the fact that she'd won three Best Actress Awards in the past, she participated as a presenter. In giving a Special Oscar to her friend Lawrence Weingarten, she admitted: "I'm living proof that someone can wait forty-one years to be unselfish . . ."

11. MARY PICKFORD, 1975

    Long a recluse, legendary silent screen star Pickford was persuaded to be filmed accepting a Special Oscar for use on the telecast of the forty-eighth Oscar ceremony. Many later felt that this was an intrusion on her

Oscar winner Fredric March fondles the reluctantly willing Miriam Hopkins in this censored still from *Dr. Jekyll and Mr. Hyde* (1931).

privacy—and her legend. The actress, then eighty-three, was not shown to advantage, but was the focus of all eyes and attention as she told Walter Mirisch: "You have made me very, very happy." It was one of Oscar's most curious, and discussed, acceptance speeches.

12. DONALD OGDEN STEWART, 1940

After listening all evening to winners thank others for their inspiration and help in getting to the winner's circle, he made a tongue-in-cheek acceptance speech for his award for *The Philadelphia Story* screenplay: "There is so much niceness here tonight that I am happy to say that I am entirely—and solely—responsible for the success of *The Philadelphia Story.*"

13 STAR QUOTES ABOUT SUCCESS AND WINNING

1. BETTE MIDLER

"Oh, please, oh, please don't let me become a pompous ass . . . anything but that."

2. BURT REYNOLDS

"I've become the number-one box-office star in the world not *because* of my pictures, but in spite of them. These were movies the critics told people they'd be fools to see, but people went to see them anyway."

3. JON VOIGHT

"I am looking forward to a time when I can handle success like it's a kind of silly friend who follows me around."

4. GEORGE BURNS

"I still get up at 8:00, I still brush my teeth with my right hand (sometimes I use my brush), I still do my exercises, I still drive the same car, I still live in the same house, I still put my coat on with my right hand and put my hair on with my left hand. So you see, everything is exactly the same as it used to be."

5. MICHAEL CAINE

"Supposing . . . all your dreams came true. Everything came true. And then you had some more . . . even more ambitious dreams. And they came true. Everything. That's the most extraordinary thing about my life. I did everything I wanted to do. Everything. I didn't miss a trick."

6. SALLY FIELD

"What hurts sometimes is that it may seem to Burt's [Reynolds] fans that I owe my success to going with him. Only I know how hard I've worked to earn my success."

7. MERYL STREEP

"I have always regarded myself as the pillar in my life."

8. ROY SCHEIDER

"I'm an overnight success. . . . only because I'm a survivor of twenty years in show business."

9. DUSTIN HOFFMAN

"I *plummeted* to stardom. . . . and it's a little like drinking strained orange juice. Being a celebrity removes the pulp from life. . . . You lose a lot of nutrients."

10. MARTIN SHEEN

"I'm really stupid. I can't spell. I get a bill and I can't figure out what the hell it means. But I always knew what I wanted. . . . I'm damn lucky, man, to be sought after to work at something that can be fun and that I can enjoy."

11. JOHN BARRYMORE

"I've done everything I ever wanted to do. I've played Hamlet. I've had every woman I ever wanted. I have a son to carry on my name. I'm bored and I'm tired."

12. BETTE DAVIS

"So I never worked with Cooper, Gable, Grant—any of the real kings of the screen. They had their films and I had mine."

13. RUTH GORDON

"To have a career, you've got to be selfish, put the blinders on, no question about it. And after you've made it you can't very well go back and help the people you've stepped on, but you can help somebody."

ROBERT OSBORNE'S LIST OF THE 4 MOST NOMINATED NONWINNERS

1. THE TURNING POINT

Setting a record in 1977, *The Turning Point* was nominated for eleven Academy Awards, including Best Picture, but failed to win a single Oscar when the final count was in. It is the most nominated nonwinner of all time.

2. RICHARD BURTON

Among actors, Burton is the most nominated nonwinner. He has been nominated seven times: *My Cousin Rachel* (1952), *The Robe* (1953), *The Spy Who Came in From the Cold* (1965), *Who's Afraid of Virginia Woolf?* (1966), *Anne of a Thousand Days* (1970), and *Equus* (1979). But he has never won.

3. DEBORAH KERR, GERALDINE PAGE, THELMA RITTER

It's a three-way tie among the ladies for being the most nominated nonwinner. Each has six nominations to her credit, without a single win among them. Their nominations:

Deborah Kerr: *Edward, My Son* (1949), *From Here to Eternity* (1953), *The King and I* (1956), *Heaven Knows, Mr. Allison* (1957), *Separate Tables* (1958), and *The Sundowners* (1960).

Geraldine Page: *Hondo* (1953), *Summer and Smoke* (1961), *Sweet*

Olivia de Havilland, Audrey Dalton, and Richard Burton in *My Cousin Rachel* (1952), for which Burton received his first of seven nonwinning Oscar nominations.

Bird of Youth (1962), *You're a Big Boy Now* (1966), *Pete 'n' Tillie* (1972), and *Interiors* (1978).

Thelma Ritter: *All About Eve* (1950), *The Mating Season* (1951), *With a Song in My Heart* (1952), *Pickup on South Street* (1953), *Pillow Talk* (1959), and *Bird Man of Alcatraz* (1962).

4. CLARENCE BROWN, KING VIDOR, ALFRED HITCHCOCK

Among directors, it's also a three-way tie with *five* nominations each; however, two have received honorary awards. In 1978, King Vidor was voted a Special Oscar for his contributions, and earlier, in 1967, Alfred Hitchcock had been voted the Irving Thalberg Award for continued excellence. Special Awards discounted, none of the three, deserving as they seem, actually won an Oscar in the annual sweepstakes. Their nominations were:

Clarence Brown: *Anna Christie* and *Romance* (1930), *A Free Soul*

(1931), *The Human Comedy* (1943), *National Velvet* (1945), and *The Yearling* (1946).

King Vidor: *The Crowd* (1928), *Hallelujah* (1930), *The Champ* (1932), *The Citadel* (1938), and *War and Peace* (1956).

Alfred Hitchcock: *Rebecca* (1940), *Lifeboat* (1944), *Spellbound* (1945), *Rear Window* (1954), and *Psycho* (1960).

25 MAJOR STARS WHO HAVE NOT WON AN OSCAR

1. KIRK DOUGLAS
2. HENRY FONDA
3. ERROL FLYNN*
4. ROBERT MITCHUM
5. PAUL NEWMAN
6. RICHARD BURTON
7. ROBERT REDFORD
8. CLINT EASTWOOD*
9. BURT REYNOLDS*
10. AL PACINO
11. MARILYN MONROE*
12. MAE WEST*
13. W. C. FIELDS*
14. MARLENE DIETRICH
15. GLORIA SWANSON
16. DEBORAH KERR
17. SHIRLEY MacLAINE
18. DORIS DAY
19. ROCK HUDSON
20. CHARLES BRONSON*
21. JEAN HARLOW*
22. MONTGOMERY CLIFT
23. WARREN BEATTY
24. JUDY GARLAND
25. MYRNA LOY*

* The stars indicated with asterisks have never been nominated for an Academy Award.

Henry Fonda (here shown with Dorris Bowden from *Grapes of Wrath* in 1940) is one of two dozen Hollywood all-time great stars who have not won an Oscar.

LIST OF POLISH FILMS TO WIN OSCAR AS BEST FOREIGN PICTURE

LIST OF 5 POLISH FILMS TO BE NOMINATED AS BEST FOREIGN PICTURE

1. KNIFE IN THE WATER (1963)
2. PHARAOH (1966)
3. THE DELUGE (1974)
4. LAND OF PROMISE (1975)
5. NIGHTS AND DAYS (1976)

ROBERT OSBORNE'S LIST OF 25 OSCAR FIRSTS

1. The First ACADEMY AWARD PRESENTATION
   May 16, 1929.
2. The First OSCAR MASTER-OF-CEREMONIES
   Douglas Fairbanks, Sr.
3. The First POSTHUMOUS WINNER
   Sidney Howard, for screenwriting *Gone With the Wind* (1939). He died August 23, 1939, in a farm accident.
4. The First REFUSAL OF AN OSCAR
   Dudley Nichols, who won for his screenplay of *The Informer;* he declined the award, he said, not to demean the honor but because of a union boycott of the 1935 Awards Ceremony.
5. The First OSCAR COVERAGE ON THE RADIO
   1928–29 ceremony on April 3, 1930, over Los Angeles KNX radio for one hour. It was the second presentation.
6. The First OSCAR TELECAST
   March 19, 1953, via NBC-TV, from the RKO Pantages Theatre in Hollywood.
7. The First COLOR OSCAR TELECAST
   April 18, 1966, via ABC-TV, from the Santa Monica Civic Auditorium.

Barbra Streisand, with her Oscar for her *first* film, *Funny Girl* (1968). She tied with Katharine Hepburn, who was awarded her third Oscar for her performance in *Lion in Winter*. Upon accepting, Streisand cooed: "Hello, gorgeous."

8. The First PERFORMER TO WIN A SECOND OSCAR—and the First to Win Consecutive Oscars:
Luise Rainer—in 1936 for *The Great Ziegfeld* and in 1937 for *The Good Earth*.

9. The First 3-TIME WINNER AMONG PERFORMERS:
Walter Brennan, as Best Supporting Actor, for *Come and Get It* (1936), *Kentucky* (1938), and *The Westerner* (1940).

10. The First RECALLED OSCAR:
In 1968, when *The Young Americans* documentary winner was declared ineligible after the fact.

11. The first X-RATED FILM TO WIN BEST PICTURE:
Midnight Cowboy (1969) (it's since been rerated).

12. The First BEST SONG WINNER
"The Continental," from *Flying Down to Rio* (1934).

13. The First ACTOR TO DIRECT HIMSELF INTO AN OSCAR NOMINATION
Charlie Chaplin in 1927 for *The Circus*.

14. The First ACTOR TO DIRECT HIMSELF INTO AN OSCAR WIN
Laurence Olivier in 1948 for *Hamlet*.

15. The First SOUND FILM TO WIN BEST PICTURE
The Broadway Melody (1928).

16. The First SUPPORTING WINNERS
Walter Brennan (for *Come and Get It*) and Gale Sondergaard (for *Anthony Adverse*) in 1936; before that, supporting performances were in the same category with starring performances.

17. The First PERSON TO WIN 4 NOMINATIONS IN A SINGLE YEAR
Orson Welles, in 1941, for *Citizen Kane:* as producer, director, actor, and screenwriter. (He won only the Best Screenplay Oscar.)

18. The First FILM TO WIN THE BIG 4 OSCARS: Best Picture, Best Actor, Best Actress, and Best Director
It Happened One Night (1934). (It also won Best Adapted Screenplay.)

19. The First FILM TO WIN 3 AWARDS FOR ACTING
In 1951, *A Streetcar Named Desire* had: Best Actress, Vivien Leigh; Best Supporting Actress, Kim Hunter; and Best Supporting Actor, Karl Malden. (Marlon Brando lost to Humphrey Bogart for *African Queen*.)

20. The First BEST PICTURE IN COLOR
Gone With the Wind (1939).

21. The First REMAKE TO WIN AS BEST PICTURE
Gigi (1958), which had been previously film in France as a nonmusical in 1950.

22. The First SEQUEL TO WIN AS BEST PICTURE
The Godfather, Part II, the 1974 follow-up to *The Godfather,* which had won Best Picture in 1972.

23. The First PERFORMER TO WIN IN A SUBTITLED ROLE

Sophia Loren won Best Actress in 1961 for *Two Women,* the first performance to win an Oscar in a foreign language.

24. The First WOMAN NOMINATED AS BEST DIRECTOR
Lina Wertmuller for *Seven Beauties* (1976).

25. The First TWO ACTORS TO WIN OSCARS FOR PLAYING THE SAME ROLE
Marlon Brando and Robert De Niro both won Oscars as Best Actor for playing Vito Corleone; Brando in 1972 in *The Godfather,* and De Niro two years later in *The Godfather, Part II.*

3 GREAT EXPECTATIONS

Or: *Howcum Our Golden Goose Laid an Egg at the Box Office?*

CHAPTER

THE TOP 40 MONEY-MAKING FILMS OF ALL TIME

The following films are the box-office champs of all time. Their earnings here reflect only rentals actually returned to the distribution company or studio from theatres in the U.S. and Canada. Foreign revenues are not included. Actual dollars taken in at the box office may be as high as double the figures on this list.

	TITLE	EARNINGS (in millions)
1.	STAR WARS (1977)	$176
2.	JAWS (1975)	$133
3.	THE EMPIRE STRIKES BACK (1980)	$120
4.	GREASE (1978)	$96
5.	THE EXORCIST (1973)	$88
6.	THE GODFATHER (1972)	$86
7.	SUPERMAN (1978)	$85
8.	THE SOUND OF MUSIC (1965)	$80
9.	THE STING (1973)	$79
10.	CLOSE ENCOUNTERS OF THE THIRD KIND (1977)	$78
11.	GONE WITH THE WIND (1939)	$77
12.	SATURDAY NIGHT FEVER (1977)	$75
13.	ANIMAL HOUSE (1978)	$74

Star Wars (1977), with Mark Hamill, Harrison Ford, Peter Mayhew (as Chewbacca), and Carrie Fisher, is the highest money-making film in Hollywood history.

Clark Gable and Vivien Leigh in their best-remembered roles as Rhett Butler and Scarlett O'Hara in *Gone With the Wind*.

14. SMOKEY AND THE BANDIT (1977) $61
15. KRAMER VS. KRAMER (1979) $61
16. ONE FLEW OVER THE CUCKOO'S NEST (1975) $59
17. STAR TREK (1980) $56
18. AMERICAN GRAFFITI (1973) $56
19. JAWS II (1978) $56
20. ROCKY (1976) $54
21. EVERY WHICH WAY BUT LOOSE (1979) $52
22. LOVE STORY (1970) $50
23. TOWERING INFERNO (1975) $50
24. THE GRADUATE (1968) $49
25. HEAVEN CAN WAIT (1978) $48
26. DOCTOR ZHIVAGO (1965) $47
27. BUTCH CASSIDY AND THE SUNDANCE KID (1969) $46
28. AIRPORT (1970) $45
29. BLAZING SADDLES (1974) $45
30. MARY POPPINS (1964) $45
31. ROCKY II (1979) $44
32. THE TEN COMMANDMENTS (1956) $43
33. THE JERK (1980) $43
34. THE POSEIDON ADVENTURE (1972) $42
35. THE GOODBYE GIRL (1977) $41
36. FIDDLER ON THE ROOF (1971) $40
37. ALIEN (1979) $40
38. YOUNG FRANKENSTEIN (1975) $39
39. SMOKEY AND THE BANDIT II (1980) $38
40. AIRPLANE (1980) $35

THE 10 HIGHEST-GROSSING FILMS IN HONG KONG

For an eclectic peek into how the other side of the world lives—and goes to the movies—let's just sample the most popularly attended films in Hong Kong for the nine-month period of January through August of 1980. The following list not only reveals the special tastes of the Hong Kong audience, but also gives a small indication of which American films seem to have international appeal. For curiosity's sake, each film's gross in Hong Kong dollars is also included. (A Hong Kong dollar is roughly equivalent to 20 cents U.S.)

1. THE YOUNG MASTER $11,059,063
   (Cantonese Kung Fu action-comedy)
2. RISING SUN $9,429,871
   (Chinese war documentary)

3.	FACES OF DEATH	$5,181,337
	(Hong Kong documentary)	
4.	KRAMER VS. KRAMER	$4,307,267
	(Family drama)	
5.	FROM RICHES TO RAGS	$4,156,174
	(Cantonese comedy)	
6.	FIST OF FURY	$4,146,687
	(Bruce Lee Kung Fu Reissue)	
7.	DISCO BUMPKINS	$4,076,741
	(Cantonese musical comedy)	
8.	AIRPORT '80—THE CONCORDE	$3,810,562
	(Disaster genre)	
9.	1941	$3,762,254
	(Disaster comedy)	
10.	ANIMALYMPICS	$3,685,554
	(Animated cartoon)	

THE TOP MONEY-MAKING FILM FOR EACH YEAR OF THE LAST 2 DECADES

Each year, one film outperforms all others at the box office. Here are the top grossers for each year, from 1960 through 1980, followed by the film rental dollars actually returned to the distribution company in Hollywood from the theatres in the U.S. and Canada, in that calendar year.

YEAR	TITLE	EARNINGS
1960	BEN-HUR	$17,300,000
1961	GUNS OF NAVARONE	8,600,000
1962	SPARTACUS	13,500,000
1963	CLEOPATRA	15,700,000
1964	THE CARPETBAGGERS	13,000,000
1965	MARY POPPINS	28,500,000
1966	THUNDERBALL	26,000,000
1967	THE DIRTY DOZEN	18,200,000
1968	THE GRADUATE	39,000,000
1969	THE LOVE BUG	17,000,000
1970	AIRPORT	37,650,800
1971	LOVE STORY	50,000,000
1972	THE GODFATHER	81,500,000
1973	THE POSEIDON ADVENTURE	40,000,000
1974	THE STING	68,450,000
1975	JAWS	102,650,000

Ben-Hur, with Charlton Heston in the title role and Stephen Boyd as Messala, was the biggest box-office attraction in 1960, earning over $17 million. The film went on to gross nearly $37 million domestically.

1976	ONE FLEW OVER THE CUCKOO'S NEST	56,500,000
1977	STAR WARS	127,000,000
1978	GREASE	83,091,000
1979	SUPERMAN	81,000,000
1980	THE EMPIRE STRIKES BACK	120,000,000

THE TOP 10 BOX-OFFICE STARS IN THE GOLDEN DECADE OF 1936–45 IN THE GOLDEN AGE OF HOLLYWOOD

1936
1. SHIRLEY TEMPLE
2. CLARK GABLE
3. GINGER ROGERS AND FRED ASTAIRE
4. ROBERT TAYLOR
5. JOE E. BROWN
6. DICK POWELL
7. JOAN CRAWFORD
8. CLAUDETTE COLBERT
9. JEANETTE MacDONALD
10. GARY COOPER

1937
1. SHIRLEY TEMPLE
2. CLARK GABLE
3. ROBERT TAYLOR
4. BING CROSBY
5. WILLIAM POWELL
6. JANE WITHERS
7. GINGER ROGERS AND FRED ASTAIRE
8. SONJA HENIE
9. GARY COOPER
10. MYRNA LOY

1938
1. SHIRLEY TEMPLE
2. CLARK GABLE
3. SONJA HENIE
4. MICKEY ROONEY
5. SPENCER TRACY
6. ROBERT TAYLOR
7. MYRNA LOY
8. JANE WITHERS
9. ALICE FAYE
10. TYRONE POWER

1939
1. MICKEY ROONEY
2. TYRONE POWER
3. SPENCER TRACY
4. CLARK GABLE
5. SHIRLEY TEMPLE
6. BETTE DAVIS
7. ALICE FAYE
8. ERROL FLYNN
9. JAMES CAGNEY
10. SONJA HENIE

1940
1. MICKEY ROONEY
2. SPENCER TRACY
3. CLARK GABLE
4. GENE AUTRY
5. TYRONE POWER
6. JAMES CAGNEY
7. BING CROSBY
8. WALLACE BEERY
9. BETTE DAVIS
10. JUDY GARLAND

1941
1. MICKEY ROONEY
2. CLARK GABLE
3. ABBOTT AND COSTELLO
4. BOB HOPE
5. SPENCER TRACY
6. GENE AUTRY
7. GARY COOPER
8. BETTE DAVIS
9. JAMES CAGNEY
10. JUDY GARLAND

Strange as it may seem, Mickey Rooney was a bigger attraction at the box office than Judy Garland in Hollywood's heyday. In fact, in the years of 1940 and 1941, he was the number one box-office draw, a plateau Garland never achieved. Here, they're seen costarring in *Andy Hardy Meets Debutante* (1940) with Betsy Booth.

1942

1. ABBOTT AND COSTELLO
2. CLARK GABLE
3. GARY COOPER
4. MICKEY ROONEY
5. BOB HOPE
6. JAMES CAGNEY
7. GENE AUTRY
8. BETTY GRABLE
9. GREER GARSON
10. SPENCER TRACY

1943

1. BETTY GRABLE
2. BOB HOPE
3. ABBOTT AND COSTELLO
4. BING CROSBY
5. GARY COOPER
6. GREER GARSON
7. HUMPHREY BOGART
8. JAMES CAGNEY
9. MICKEY ROONEY
10. CLARK GABLE

1944

1. BING CROSBY
2. GARY COOPER
3. BOB HOPE
4. BETTY GRABLE
5. SPENCER TRACY
6. GREER GARSON
7. HUMPHREY BOGART
8. ABBOTT AND COSTELLO
9. CARY GRANT
10. BETTE DAVIS

1945

1. BING CROSBY
2. VAN JOHNSON
3. GREER GARSON
4. BETTY GRABLE
5. SPENCER TRACY
6. GARY COOPER,
   HUMPHREY BOGART
7. BOB HOPE
8. JUDY GARLAND
9. MARGARET O'BRIEN
10. ROY ROGERS

THE SALARIES OF 15 MOVIE SUPERSTARS

In the Golden Age of Hollywood, MGM used to boast that it had more stars than there are in heaven. Today the superstars boast that they're getting more bucks than there are stars in the heavens. Ten years ago, a $1 million fee for a star was unheard of. Five years ago, perhaps a handful of stars could demand—and get—that kind of money. But in the 1980s, as clear a yardstick of inflation as you can find, there are several dozen big-name actors who draw such a salary regularly.

1. CHARLIE CHAPLIN
   In 1917, Chaplin was the highest-paid silent screen star. The first genuine superstar of the movies, he was paid $1 million to direct and star in eight two-reel comedies, plus a bonus of $15,000 for each reel over two, and fifty percent of the profits on all over five reels. It was an enormous amount of money for those days.

2. GRETA GARBO

In the mid-thirties, while under contract to MGM, she was paid $300,000 per film. She was the first genuine female superstar and commanded the money to prove it.

3. MARLENE DIETRICH

In 1937, she was paid $450,000 for *Knight Without Armor,* which made her the highest-paid woman in the world for the year.

4. HUMPHREY BOGART

In the mid-fifties, Bogart commanded a quarter of a million per film, making him the highest-paid freelance actor of his day. Bogart said then: "What makes me think I'm worth $250,000 per picture? Because I can get it." He set the trend toward rising salaries based on supply and demand.

5. STEVE McQUEEN

His asking price was $5 million for a film. Although on the announced, but halted, *Taipan,* he was to get a reported $10 million . . . plus a percentage . . . making him the most expensive superstar ever.

6. SYLVESTER STALLONE

He contracted for $7 million to write, direct, and star in *Rocky III.* But he had asked for $10 million.

7. BURT REYNOLDS

Many consider him to be the number-one box-office attraction in the world—in a close tie with Clint Eastwood—and he easily commands $3 million per film, plus ten percent of the gross profits.

8. DUSTIN HOFFMAN

He's graduated to the same price category.

9. MARLON BRANDO

He gets $3 million per picture plus a percentage, which is what he was paid for *Superman* . . . and it remains a mystery to many why he was given that kind of money for a glorified cameo.

10. PAUL NEWMAN

His price is $3 million, and there's no argument. If you want Newman, or any other superstar, you pay the going rate.

11. ROBERT REDFORD

He was paid $2 million for a featured role in *A Bridge Too Far* in 1977. Said Redford: "It's hard to turn down that kind of money, and yet I think it's ridiculous for a producer to pay it." He now commands $3 million per film.

12. BO DEREK

Her price has obviously escalated rapidly since *10,* and she's now commanding a million plus; her reported salary on *Change of Seasons* (1980) was $750,000.

13. STEVE MARTIN

He earned a half-million for his film debut in *The Jerk* (1979). The success of that hit-and-miss comedy will surely double his price.

14. FARRAH FAWCETT
    Since leaving "Charlie's Angels" in 1977, she's made three films and was reportedly paid the following sums: *Somebody Killed Her Husband* (1978), $500,000; then $750,000 for *Sunburn* (1979), which didn't do great business, so her price dropped to $450,000 for *Saturn 3* (1980).
15. CHRISTOPHER REEVE
    His price for *Superman* (1979) and *Superman II* (1981) totaled $250,000. "Which wasn't bad," says Reeve, "when they were both supposed to be wrapped up inside of ten months. But it's been over two years. I'd have made more doing TV soap opera. I did get overtime after a year on *Superman,* and they've offered me merchandising and profit participation. But it's no fortune." He now commands much more, based on the success of *Superman.*

5 SUPERSTARS IN THE MULTIMILLION-DOLLAR CATEGORY . . .

. . . who prefer to develop their properties through their own production companies and work for a huge controlling share of the profits rather than a salary:

1. CLINT EASTWOOD
    Some say he's the richest actor in the world. His films have grossed near $500 million. A little chunk of that seems wiser than a salary.
2. WOODY ALLEN
3. WARREN BEATTY
4. JANE FONDA
5. BARBRA STREISAND

11 SUPERSTARS IN THE MILLION-DOLLAR BRACKET

1. AL PACINO
2. RICHARD DREYFUSS
3. JAMES CAAN
4. ROBERT DE NIRO
5. GENE HACKMAN
6. CHARLES BRONSON
7. JON VOIGHT
8. JACK NICHOLSON
9. SEAN CONNERY
10. JOHN TRAVOLTA
11. JACQUELINE BISSET

THE TOP 10 BOX-OFFICE STARS OF THE 1950s

These are the stars selected by theatre owners around the country as the ones who consistently make them the most money. The lists for the following three decades were compiled by Quigley Publications

The ultimate screen hero, Clint Eastwood, striking a characteristically stoic pose in *Bronco Billy* (1980), was the top box-office attraction for the decade of the 1970s. He's still number one.

from their annual polls. Interestingly, male stars dominate 80 percent of the lists. Historically, actresses do not command the box-office draw of leading men.

1. JOHN WAYNE
2. JAMES STEWART
3. GARY COOPER
4. BING CROSBY
5. DEAN MARTIN and JERRY LEWIS
6. BOB HOPE
7. FRANK SINATRA
8. WILLIAM HOLDEN
9. RANDOLPH SCOTT
10. MARILYN MONROE

THE TOP 10 BOX-OFFICE STARS OF THE 1960s

1. JOHN WAYNE
2. ELIZABETH TAYLOR
3. DORIS DAY
4. PAUL NEWMAN
5. JACK LEMMON
6. ELVIS PRESLEY
7. ROCK HUDSON
8. JULIE ANDREWS
9. RICHARD BURTON
10. SANDRA DEE

THE TOP 10 BOX OFFICE STARS OF THE 1970s

1. CLINT EASTWOOD
2. STEVE McQUEEN
3. PAUL NEWMAN
4. BARBRA STREISAND
5. JOHN WAYNE
6. ROBERT REDFORD
7. CHARLES BRONSON
8. BURT REYNOLDS
9. WOODY ALLEN
10. AL PACINO

14 STARS ON THE CALIFORNIA STATE CONTROLLER'S HOLDING LIST

State Controller Ken Corey announced in October 1980 that fourteen stars' names turned up on a list of "bank funds being held by the state as unclaimed property." Each year the State Controller's office returns about $30 million in such money to owners who let it languish too long in savings and checking accounts, uncashed traveler's checks, money orders, etc. Here are the fourteen stars who have money being held for them by the state of California:

1. GRETA GARBO, $41.04
2. MARION DAVIES, $25.00
3. LILLI PALMER, $39.90
4. GENE BARRY, $40.00
5. JAMES BROLIN, $73.39
6. DYAN CANNON, $51.11
7. BILL COSBY, $234.08
8. KATE JACKSON, $55.00
9. ART LINKLETTER, $167.70
10. JAMES MASON, $63.00
11. VERA MILES, $425.00
12. SIMONE SIGNORET, $87.87
13. PETER USTINOV, $92.60
14. ROBERT VAUGHN, $69.81

Greta Garbo uttered her first words from the screen in *Anna Christie* (1930): "Gif me a viskey, ginger ale on the side...an' don't be stingy, baby."

21 FAMOUS AD LINES MATCH-UP QUIZ

If you figured that somewhere along the way, you'd have a chance to show your nostalgia knowledge, you've come to the right page. Here is the first of three such trivia teasers. This one deals with movie slogan ad lines that became almost as famous as the movies themselves.

For example: *"Garbo talks!"* was the simple slogan that advertised *Anna Christie*, Greta Garbo's first talkie (1930); It brought her fans to the theatres in droves. The first words uttered by the legendary star from the screen were: "Gif me a viskey, ginger ale on the side . . . an' don't be stingy, baby."

Now match up these famous slogans with their respective films:

1. In space no one can hear you scream.
2. Gable's back . . . and Garson's got him.
3. Just when you thought it was safe to go back in the water.
4. The beauty and the beast.
5. The night *he* came back.
6. A glove story.
7. The monster demands a mate.
8. His whole life was a million-to-one shot.
9. They're young . . . they're in love . . . and they kill people.
10. We are not alone . . .
11. The strangest passion the world has ever known.
12. It is unlikely you will ever experience in a lifetime all that you'll see in . . .
13. A man went looking for America. And couldn't find it anywhere.
14. No one . . . but no one . . . will be admitted to the theatre after the start of each performance of . . .
15. You will believe a man can fly.
16. Love means never having to say you're sorry.
17. All it takes is a little confidence.
18. If this story ain't true . . . it shoulda been.
19. Some films you watch. Others you feel.
20. We are going to eat you.
21. That's right. I made another movie. You know me. I can't stop creating.

a. ADVENTURE (1945)
b. ALIEN (1979)
c. BONNIE AND CLYDE (1967)
d. BRIDE OF FRANKENSTEIN (1935)
e. THE CARPETBAGGERS (1964)
f. CLOSE ENCOUNTERS OF THE THIRD KIND (1977)
g. DRACULA (1931)
h. EASY RIDER (1969)
i. HALLOWEEN (1978)
j. JAWS II (1979)
k. KING KONG (1976)
l. THE LIFE AND TIMES OF JUDGE ROY BEAN (1972)
m. LOVE STORY (1970)
n. THE MAIN EVENT (1979)
o. OH GOD! BOOK II (1980)
p. ORDINARY PEOPLE (1980)
q. PSYCHO (1960)
r. ROCKY (1976)
s. THE STING (1973)
t. SUPERMAN (1979)
u. ZOMBIE (1980)

10 UNFORGETTABLE LINES OF DIALOGUE
FROM THE MOVIES

1. "Do you mind if I change into something more comfortable?"

   Jean Harlow to Ben Lyon in *Hell's Angels* (1930). Lyon didn't mind. And neither did the public. Harlow's seduction scene in this film made her a star.

2. "I vant to be alone."

   Greta Garbo to John Barrymore in *Grand Hotel* (1932). She repeated the line several times in the picture, and it became a permanent part of her image. In years since, she has told reporters that what she really wanted was "to be left alone. There's a difference."

3. "Frankly, my dear, I don't give a damn!"

   Clark Gable as Rhett Butler to Vivien Leigh as Scarlett O'Hara in *Gone With the Wind* (1939). This, the most famous line of dialogue from any motion picture, introduced swearing to the cinema; the picture was condemned by the Catholic Legion of Decency, making it a mortal sin for Catholics to see the film in its initial run.

4. "But, Miss Scarlett, I don't know nuthin' about birthin' no babies."

   Butterfly McQueen to Vivien Leigh in, you guessed it, *Gone With the Wind*.

5. "If you want anything just whistle. You know how to whistle, don't you? You just put your lips together and blow."

   Lauren Bacall to Humphrey Bogart in *To Have and Have Not* (1944). Bogart whistled, and kept right on whistling.

7. "What we have here is a failure to communicate."

   Strother Martin to Paul Newman in *Cool Hand Luke* (1967).

8. "Love means never having to say you're sorry."

   Ali MacGraw to Ryan O'Neal in *Love Story* (1970). Although one of movies' most famous lines, it is also extremely enigmatic. No one has really been able to figure out what it means. Love, I would think, means rather a willingness to say you're sorry when you've been a fool.

9. "I'll make him an offer he can't refuse."

   Marlon Brando to Robert Duvall in *Godfather* (1972); Al Pacino to

Robert Duvall in *Godfather II* (1974); Francis Ford Coppola to Mario Puzo about Brando for *Godfather;* Ilya Salkind to Richard Donner about Brando for *Superman;* Francis Ford Coppola about Brando for *Apocalypse Now!*

10. "The Force be with you."

Alec Guinness as Ben Kenobi to Mark Hamill as Luke Skywalker in *Star Wars* (1977), the most popular flight of fantasy ever put on the screen.

5 FAMOUS LINES THAT WERE NEVER SAID IN THE MOVIES

1. "Smile, when you say that, pardner."

What Gary Cooper actually said to Walter Huston in *The Virginian* (1929), was: "If you want to call me that, smile." But the line was misquoted from the start. The publicity stills from the picture read: "When you call me that, smile."

Humphrey Bogart tells Sam (Dooley Wilson) not to play it again in *Casablanca* (1943), as Claude Rains looks on.

2. "Me Tarzan, you Jane."

   Everyone remembers Johnny Weissmuller grunting this line to Maureen O'Sullivan in *Tarzan, the Apeman* (1932). However, the actual screen delivery had Weissmuller thumping his brawny chest as he said, "Tarzan," and then thumping O'Sullivan's nubile chest as he exclaimed, "Jane."

3. "Come up and see me sometime."

   Mae West did invite Cary Grant over in *She Done Him Wrong* (1933), but her exact words in the film were: "Why don't you come up sometime and see me?" No mistaking the invitation.

4. "Come with me to the Casbah, and we'll make beautiful music together."

   Throughout most of *Algiers* (1938), Charles Boyer tried to get Hedy Lamarr to the Casbah for his romantic purposes, but he never actually said the above words. The line became notorious when people imitated Boyer, and said things which were mistaken as being from the movie.

5. "Play it again, Sam."

   In *Casablanca* (1943), Ingrid Bergman tells piano-playing Dooley Wilson to: "Play it, Sam." At which Humphrey Bogart comes over and says, "I thought I told you never to play that again." But when he notices Ingrid, he doesn't stop the music. And neither would any of us, but nobody told Sam to play it again.

# FORBIDDEN FRUIT

CHAPTER 4

Or: *How Much Cleavage Can You Show in a Family Picture?*

MAE WEST'S LIST OF A DOZEN BAWDY ONE-LINERS FROM HER FILMS

One of the genuine legends of Hollywood, the late Mae West was a sex symbol for longer than any other movie queen. She debuted in films in *Night After Night* (1932), and her last film was *Sextette* (1978), spanning over a half-century. She became famous, and infamous, for her bawdy sense of humor. In her own often-quoted words: "Sex and I have a lot in common. I don't want to take credit for inventing it—but I may say, in my own modest way, and in a manner of speaking, that I have rediscovered it." Her movie dialogue, which she always wrote, was distinctively characteristic, and more memorable and quotable than any other star's in the history of the silver screen. She was the unmatched mistress of the double entendre and the sexual innuendo. One line in particular seems to catch her full flavor: "When I'm good, I'm very, very good, but when I'm bad, I'm better."

1. "Goodness had nothing to do with it."

    The reply to the hatcheck girl, who says, "Goodness, what lovely diamonds."—*Night After Night,* 1932.

Mae West, the unmatched mistress of the double entendre, tells Randolph Scott that, "A thrill a day keeps the chills away," in *Go West, Young Man* (1936).

2. "A figure with curves always offers a lot of interesting angles."
   I'm No Angel (1933)

3. "Is that a gun in your pocket or are you just glad to see me?"
   She Done Him Wrong (1933)

4. "It's better to be looked over than to be overlooked."
   Belle of the Nineties (1934)

5. "Don't make the same mistake twice—unless it pays."
   Belle of the Nineties (1934)

6. "Between two evils, I always pick the one I haven't tried before."
   Klondike Annie (1936)

7. "Give a man a free hand, and he'll put it all over you."
   Klondike Annie (1936)

8. "A thrill a day keeps the chills away."
   Go West, Young Man (1936)

9. "Anytime you got nothin' to do—and lots of time to do it—come on up."
   My Little Chickadee (1940)

10. "I always say, keep a diary, and someday it'll keep you."
    Every Day's a Holiday (1937)

11. "I generally avoid temptation, unless I can't resist it."
    My Little Chickadee (1940)

12. "It's not the men in my life, but the life in my men that counts."
    Sextette (1978)

A BAKER'S DOZEN FAMOUS FILMS BANNED IN BOSTON

Who banned them? The Catholic Legion of Decency, of course. And the Legion banned these films in Los Angeles, New York, Phoenix, Atlanta, and everywhere else.

The Catholic Legion of Decency was created in 1934 to clean up the rampant immorality and irresponsibility of the movies. Monsignor Cicognani lamented then: "What a massacre of innocence of youth is taking place hour by hour. How shall the crimes that have their direct source in immoral motion pictures be measured? Catholics are called by God and the Pope to a united and vigorous campaign for the purification of the cinema, which has become a deadly menace to our morals."

The way the Legion went about doing this was to rate films according to the following classifications:

A-1: Morally Unobjectionable for General Patronage
A-2: Morally Unobjectionable for Adults and Adolescents
A-3: Morally Unobjectionable for Adults

A-4: Adults Only, with Reservations
B: Morally Objectionable in Part for Everybody
C: Condemned

Condemned films could not be seen by Catholics without penalty of sin, since these movies were considered by the Holy Father, because of theme or treatment, to be "positively bad."

1. GONE WITH THE WIND (1939)
    This classic got a C rating automatically because of the famous line delivered by Clark Gable as Rhett Butler: "Frankly, my dear, I don't give a damn." It was considered an obscenity, and as such was morally corruptive. (A few years later, following several appeals, the rating was changed to A-4.)

2. THE OUTLAW (1941)
    The furor accompanying this picture's release was massive. The Production Code Administration (PCA), Hollywood's own censorship office, denied the film a seal of approval and managed to keep the film out of distribution from 1941 to 1943, at which time Howard Hughes, the producer/director, exhibited it briefly. The Legion lobbied exhaustively against the picture, but it reappeared in 1946 with an advertising campaign that has since become legendary: "What Are the Two Great Rea-

Howard Hughes' production of *The Outlaw* (1941) blended sex with the Western genre and made an international star of Jane Russell, whose formidable physical assets brought abundant bosoms back into vogue. Here, she prepares to perform surgery on the sleeping Jack Beutel. Censorship conflicts kept the film out of theatres for three years.

sons for Jane Russell's Rise to Stardom?" the ads asked coyly. One Baltimore judge claimed that Russell's breasts in all their magnificence "hung over the film like a thunderstorm spread out over a landscape."

3. THE MIRACLE (1951)

In this Italian import, Anna Magnani played a goat girl who gave herself to a vagrant she believed to be St. Joseph. The Legion condemned the movie and launched a major effort to have it banned in the U.S. altogether. The Supreme Court ruled that "sacrilegious" was a term too ambiguous to be enforced, and that movies were an art form protected by the freedom of the First Amendment.

4. THE MOON IS BLUE (1953)

In addition to being condemned by the Legion, this Otto Preminger film was also denied a PCA seal. The adultery theme was deemed repugnant to everybody but United Artists, which withdrew from the Producers' Association to release the movie. It drew large crowds because of the controversy, though in some small towns police actually took down the names of people who saw the film. This was the first time that a major studio made a profit with a picture that was scarred with the scarlet C.

5. THE MAN WITH THE GOLDEN ARM (1955)

This was another film by Otto Preminger that took a beating—because of its graphic depiction of drug addiction. Frank Sinatra as the man with a monkey on his back gave a devastating performance. The film was denied the PCA seal of approval. Drugs were still in the closet.

6. BABY DOLL (1956)

Cardinal Spellman warned Catholics to stay away from this film about child bride Carroll Baker's debauched innocence. Bishops even placed a six-month boycott on theatres that ran it. But the social climate was changing, and the notoriety of the film only enhanced its box-office returns.

7. AND GOD CREATED WOMAN (1957)

There was quite a furor about this film's nudity, which introduced and made a star of Brigitte Bardot. This was the first popular mainstream picture to feature so much naked flesh; tame by today's standards, but a trend setter.

8. LOLITA (1962)

This strange film by Stanley Kubrick from Nabokov's provocative novel provoked a C. Sexually precocious Sue Lyons becomes involved with stolid professor James Mason, leading to murder and lust. Garnered nearly as much criticism as *Baby Doll*.

9. THE PAWNBROKER (1966)

A milestone case for the Legion: The film was automatically condemned because of some scenes with bare breasts, and the brief nudity overshadowed the otherwise serious intent, depicting how a man, Rod Steiger, a former concentration camp victim, cannot escape his memories. The resulting self-searching within the organization led eventually to a modification of its heretofore ironclad "no nudity" rule.

10. VALLEY OF THE DOLLS (1967)
Jacqueline Susann's novel was trashy, but the movie version was an all-time low in exploitative use of graphic violence, gratuitous nudity, cynical and amoral views, and sleazy characters.

11. STRAW DOGS (1971)
Sam Peckinpah's highly controversial violence-themed picture—with gratuitously filmed rape scenes that demean women and play on the male fantasy that women invite and enjoy rape.

12. FRIDAY THE 13TH (1980)
An inexcusable exercise in mindless pornographic violence to make an exploitative buck. There's not a single frame of redeemable value.

13. DRESSED TO KILL (1980)
A perfectly loathsome little movie with fantasy sequences that seem to have sprung from the kind of fevered but impoverished male imagination that feels threatened by any woman who is neither masochist nor prostitute.

. . . AND 3 FILMS SURPRISINGLY NOT BANNED

Since the late sixties, the Legion of Decency has on the average branded 15 percent of Hollywood's annual output with a C. But, surprisingly, some of the films which you'd expect to get a C, or at least a B, rating, were given an A-4. Here are three:

1. WHO'S AFRAID OF VIRGINIA WOOLF? (1966)
This excellent Mike Nichols film with Elizabeth Taylor and Richard Burton broke a lot of Hollywood taboos about adult material and turned the air blue with foul language, but the Legion felt it was worthwhile viewing for adults, with reservations.

2. MIDNIGHT COWBOY (1969)
This Oscar-winning John Schlesinger film with Jon Voight and Dustin Hoffman was rated X, but the Legion saw it as a serious slice of life, homosexuality and all.

3. SATURDAY NIGHT FEVER (1977)
Despite the heavy usage of four-letter words and the dissolute back-seat doings, it was deemed to contain some positive moral values.

NOTE: In September, 1980, the U.S. Catholic Church closed down its film office, and with it the last remnants of the Legion of Decency. Publication of its biweekly *Review* magazine, which since 1935 has carried reviews and ratings of some 16,000 motion pictures, has ceased. The reason is financial, but the office and its service clearly fell victim to the changing times, public morality, the movie business, and the church itself. It is the end of an era and a sad comment on our social condition. We have lost a valuable watchdog.

THE HOLLYWOOD PRODUCTION CODE'S 3 MAIN PRINCIPLES

In 1934, with the formation of the Catholic Legion of Decency, Hollywood film producers banded together to prevent federal censorship which many thought would be coming because of the uproar created by the clergy.

Under the supervision of a young Catholic newspaperman, Joseph Breen, the PCA was set up as a branch of the Hays Office (which had been attempting industry self-censorship for twelve years). The PCA's code book was written by Father Daniel Lord and Martin Quigley, a prominent Catholic layman who was also a powerful publisher. It then fell to Breen to police film production and to censor unsavory or immoral material. He had the power to fine offenders $25,000 for not abiding by his rulings; and if he withheld the PCA seal of approval, most theatre chains wouldn't handle the picture in question.

The 3 general principles governing all films were laid out this way:

1. No picture shall be produced that will lower the moral standards of those who see it. Hence the sympathy of the audience shall never be thrown to the side of crime, wrongdoing, evil, or sin.
2. Correct standards of life, subject only to the requirements of drama and entertainment, shall be presented.
3. Law, natural and human, shall not be ridiculed, nor shall sympathy be created for its violation.

... AND THE PCA'S 11 "DON'TS"

"Resolved that those things which are included in the following list shall not appear in pictures produced by members of this Association, irrespective of the manner in which they are treated":

1. Pointed profanity—by either title or lip. This includes the words "God," "Lord," "Jesus," "Christ" (unless they are used reverently in connection with proper religious ceremonies), "hell," "damn," "Gawd," and every other profane and vulgar expression however it may be spelled.

2. Any licentious or suggestive nudity—in fact or in silhouette; or any lecherous or licentious notice thereof by other characters in the picture
3. The illegal traffic in drugs
4. Any inference of sex perversion
5. White slavery
6. Miscegenation [sex relationships between the white and black races]
7. Sex hygiene and venereal diseases
8. Scenes of actual childbirth—in fact or in silhouette
9. Children's sex organs
10. Ridicule of the clergy
11. Willful offense to any nation, race, or creed

... AND THE PCA'S 25 "BE CAREFULS"

"And be it further resolved that special care be exercised in the manner in which the following subjects are treated, to the end that vulgarity and suggestiveness be eliminated and that good taste be emphasized":

1. The use of the flag
2. International relations [avoiding picturizing in an unfavorable light another country's religion, history, institutions, prominent people, and citizenry]
3. Arson
4. The use of firearms
5. Theft, robbery, safe-cracking, and dynamiting of trains, mines, buildings, etc. [having in mind the effect which a too-detailed description of these may have upon the moron]
6. Brutality and possible gruesomeness
7. Technique of committing murder by whatever method
8. Methods of smuggling
9. Third-degree methods
10. Actual hangings or electrocutions as legal punishment for crime
11. Sympathy for criminals
12. Attitude toward public characters and institutions
13. Sedition
14. Apparent cruelty to children and animals
15. Branding of people or animals
16. The sale of women, or of a woman selling her virtue
17. Rape or attempted rape
18. First-night scenes
19. Man and woman in bed together
20. Deliberate seduction of girls
21. The institution of marriage
22. Surgical operations
23. The use of drugs

This famous 1940 photo cleverly illustrates ten of the major *Don't's* and *Be Careful's* of the Hollywood Production Code Administration.

24. Titles or scenes having to do with law enforcement or law enforcement officers
25. Excessive or lustful kissing, particularly when one character or the other is a "heavy"

THREE EXPERTS PICK THE TOP 10 ALL-TIME MOVIE SEX GODDESSES

Eileen Ford, head of the top New York–based Ford Modeling Agency, Richard Blackwell, leading Hollywood dress designer, and Arthur Knight, columnist, critic, and historian, compiled a list of 10 American Love Goddesses, and rated them on a scale of 1 to 10. The results:

1. MARILYN MONROE (27 points)
   Ford: "Marilyn had a special quality the others didn't have."
   Blackwell: "There was a childlike simplicity about her that appealed to a man's protective instincts."
   Knight: "Marilyn epitomized the blonde bombshell image."
2. RITA HAYWORTH (24 points)
   Blackwell: "In her, God created female perfection. She had an inner and outward sex appeal. She had everything."
3. JEAN HARLOW (20 points)
   Knight: "Harlow made it all happen. Until her, the blonde was always the good girl next door. She gave blondeness a new image, and made it sexy."
4. LANA TURNER (17 points)
   Ford: "She was the pinup queen of her generation. She became a sex goddess through her natural beauty because in those days you didn't have to bare your body to become one."
5. ANN-MARGRET (16 points)
   Knight: "She communicates sexuality with tremendous energy. There's a great animal sense about her . . . she looks like she bites."
6. RAQUEL WELCH (15 points)
   Ford: "I gave her a nine. She has a natural beauty, and though she's not the actress Monroe was, she does have charm and personality."
7. MARLENE DIETRICH (14 points)
   Blackwell: "She was a super, untouchable lady. She had the kind of sensuous appeal that never seemed attainable, but was always desirable."
8. BETTY GRABLE (13 points)
   Knight: "She always seemed like she'd be fun to know. She had that girl-next-door appeal."
9. JANE RUSSELL (11 points)
   Blackwell: "I think she was too earthy. She had a seedy sex appeal. You'd never put her on satin sheets."
10. PAULETTE GODDARD (9 points)
    Knight: "She was very vivacious. There was a great sense of fun about her, and she was considered pretty sexy with those bright eyes and come hither look."

ERICA JONG'S LIST OF MEMORABLE ZIPLESS LOVE SCENES FROM THE MOVIES

Poet and novelist Erica Jong is best known for her spicy novel *Fear of Flying* (1973), in which she identified, once and for all time, the zipless sexual encounter.

Jong: "There aren't any zipless love scenes in the movies."

MEASUREMENTS OF 7 FABULOUS FILMLAND FIGURES

NAME	BUST/WAIST/HIPS
1. BARBRA STREISAND	36-25-36
2. ANN-MARGRET	36½-25-36
3. JACQUELINE BISSET	37-25-36
4. JILL ST. JOHN	35-23½-34½
5. RAQUEL WELCH	36-24-36
6. BO DEREK	35-23½-35½
7. BETTE MIDLER	36½-25-36

... AND A FETCHING 15 FROM MEMORY LANE

NAME	BUST/WAIST/HIPS
1. MARILYN MONROE	37-23½-37
2. JANE RUSSELL	39-26½-37½
3. SHELLEY WINTERS	37-26½-36
4. AVA GARDNER	36-23½-37
5. ELIZABETH TAYLOR	36-21-36
6. RITA HAYWORTH	36½-24-36
7. JEANNE CRAIN	33½-24-36
8. CYD CHARISSE	34-23-35
9. LANA TURNER	34-25-34
10. ZSA ZSA GABOR	36-25-36
11. SUSAN HAYWARD	35-25½-35½
12. BETTY GRABLE	36-24-35
13. JAYNE MANSFIELD	39½-23-36½
14. SOPHIA LOREN	37-24½-36
15. BRIGITTE BARDOT	35-25-36

THE "THERE IS NOTHING LIKE A DAME" PHOTO-QUIZ OF 10 FAMOUS FILMLAND FIGURES

There is nothing like a dame! That's what the movies have been telling us from the time that Hollywood became a town and began peddling tinsel. And as you can see from the following photos, Hollywood has been right. And, plainly, you have stumbled onto the second quiz. The object is to figure out the identities of these ten gorgeous filmland dames from their unmistakable anatomies. Score a ten, and you are obviously a true connoisseur of celluloid feminine pulchritude.

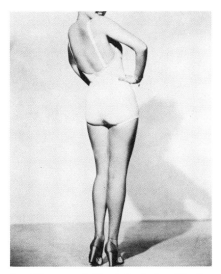

A. She was dubbed the lady with the million-dollar legs, and was one of the top three pinup queens during World War II.

B. Howard Hughes claimed to have designed an aerodynamic bras-siere for her. Whatever it was, it worked.

C. She changed her name, her hair color, and danced her way into sex symbol status as Sadie Thompson.

D. She was the sarong queen, and hit the road a half-dozen times with two famous comedians.

E. She proved bathing suits could be more than functional, and that she was dangerous when wet.

F. She was the most famous and most enigmatic sex symbol of the century, and proved that gentlemen do indeed prefer blondes.

G. Though winning a beauty contest brought her to Hollywood, she denied it for years to be taken seriously as an actress.

H. She was the girl who couldn't help it, and became the ultimate blonde bombshell.

I. Her sultry sexiness inspired desire under the elms on an international level.

J. With her perfect figure eight, she bedazzled male moviegoers everywhere.

ANSWERS

J. Raquel Welch I. Sophia Loren H. Jayne Mansfield G. Vera Miles F. Marilyn Monroe

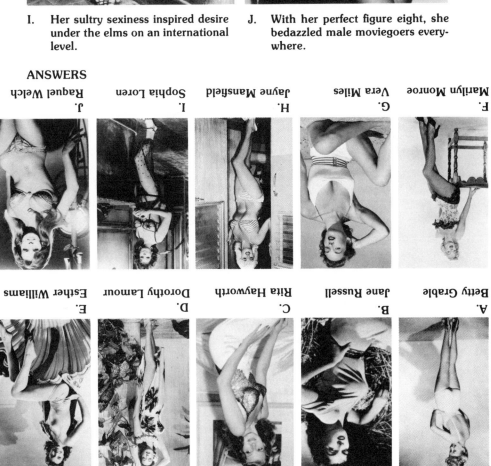

E. Esther Williams D. Dorothy Lamour C. Rita Hayworth B. Jane Russell A. Betty Grable

77

4 MOVIES ABOUT SEX CHANGE

1. HOMICIDAL (1961)
   Director: William Castle; Glenn Corbet. A gimmick thriller which pivots on a sex change.
2. MYRA BRECKENRIDGE (1970)
   Director: Michael Sarne; Mae West, John Huston, Farrah Fawcett. Raquel Welch and Rex Reed play the same role in this tasteless version of Gore Vidal's seriocomic camp novel of sex change.
3. THE CHRISTINE JORGENSON STORY (1970)
   Director: Irving Rapper. Hoping to ride through on the tails of *Myra Breckenridge,* this ludicrous bomb exploited the famed real-life '50s case.
4. I WANT WHAT I WANT (1972)
   Director: John Dexter; Anne Heywood. This British entry tries earnestly enough, but has difficulty not smirking slightly about its subject matter.

MAN WATCHERS, INC. LISTS 10 ALL-TIME MOVIE WATCHABLES

In 1975, Burt Reynolds was targeted as the numero uno watchable male star by Man Watchers, Inc. According to Suzy Mallery, president and founder of Man Watchers, he was chosen for his "animal magnetism, masculinity, sense of humor, and great good looks—from top to bottom."

An international organization with over 2,000 members in the U.S., Canada, England, and Australia, Man Watchers conducts annual polls about which men are well worth watching. And when a member happens upon a guy who deserves an ogle or two, she lays a "Well Worth Watching" card on his person to let him know that he's been ogled by a pro.

Says Mallery: "We try not to be too obvious. The dirty sunglasses technique works very well. You remove your glasses, and hold them out as if to check them for dirt. This gives you a chance to look the man over, and he'll never be the wiser."

Here are some of the Movie Males who've had the dirty sunglasses trick done on them a few more times than the average guy.

1. BURT REYNOLDS
   We love his sense of humor, the twinkle in his eye.
2. JAMES CAAN
   He's mucho macho, has a great body and a cheerful restlessness.
3. ROBERT REDFORD

Suzy Mallery (with trophy) and members of Men Watchers, Inc., present the "Well Worth Watching" Award to Burt Reynolds at Paramount Studios in 1975.

Traditionally handsome, with a boyish all-American charm.

4. PAUL NEWMAN

Beautiful blue eyes, strong masculine features, great mouth.

5. JAMES GARNER

Good looking, charming, and appeals to women of all ages.

6. CLINT EASTWOOD

Finely etched, chiseled good looks.

7. CARY GRANT

Distinguished, urbane, a silver fox.

8. JACK NICHOLSON

A killer smile, and cobra eyes.

9. O. J. SIMPSON

Very handsome and well built.

10. MICHAEL CAINE

Suave and sexy in a cosmopolitan way.

...AND 3 HOLIDAY TURKEYS (WHO SHOULD CLEAN UP THEIR ACTS)

1. EVIL KNEVIL

... for his overuse of a baseball bat.

2. JIMMY CONNORS

... for bad manners and obscene gestures on a tennis court.

3. BILLY CARTER

... for bad judgment, bad taste, and careless grooming.

5

CHAPTER

THE SECRET LIFE OF WALTER MITTY

Or: *How Private Can an Actor's Private Life Be?*

ROBERT STACK'S LIST OF THE 11 TOP SKEET SHOOTERS IN HOLLYWOOD'S HEYDAY

In the decade before World War II, the Golden Era of Hollywood, when movies were as much glamour as they were a business, the big stars played at the games of kings, which were often as much a sign of social status as a sport in themselves. Such things as polo and skeet shooting were particular favorites.

Says Stack: "When I was growing up in Hollywood, skeet shooting was *the* sport of the stars. I wasn't a colleague of the stars I shot with, because I was just a kid of sixteen, mingling with the giants like Cooper, Gable, and Howard Hughes. Gable was almost my proxy father, in a way. I was a giant only in the sense that, at the time, I was an All-American shooter and held two world records. My hottest year was when I was seventeen in 1936. I was All-American, I broke the Long Run Skeet record, we broke the Five-Man Team record, and I won every major tournament except for the National, and I was runner-up in that. The only irony was that one of the old shooters later said to me, 'You hit your peak by the time you were eighteen. From then on it was downhill; you went into acting.' "

Robert Stack made his film debut in *First Love* (1939) and gave Deanna Durbin (one of the most asked-about stars of yesteryear) her first screen kiss.

1. CLARK GABLE
   "My duck hunting partner, and a great friend; a good skeet shot but better on ducks."
2. ROBERT TAYLOR
   "A real outdoorsman; he could do it all."
3. ANDY DEVINE
   "He was one of Hollywood's best skeet shooters."
4. FRED MacMURRAY
   "He was the best of the skeet-shooting actors. He shot well enough to shoot alternate on our World Record Five-Man Team. When one of the guys got sick, Fred shot three great scores for us, winding up the last score with 100 out of 100. Then he put down his gun and never fired again because the pressure was too great on him. He said, 'I know I'm gonna fall apart on you and ruin the team.' So he quit. But he quit at the top."
5. HOWARD HUGHES
   "He always booked a private field, and always brought along a beautiful dame."
6,7. WARD BOND and JOHN WAYNE
   "They usually came out together; both loved hunting and fishing. Duke

once shot him in the back by accident. Bond starts yelling, 'I'm shot! I'm shot!' Duke walks over and rips Bond's shirt off, and says, 'This gun of mine sure throws a good pattern.' "

8. GARY COOPER

"He was a better rifle shot than with a shotgun; he was companion to Hemingway on many hunting expeditions."

9. ERNEST HEMINGWAY

"A good skeet shot, and an outstanding live bird shot. He used to go to Cuba in the old days, before Castro."

10. JOHN BARRYMORE

"He had his own skeet field, but he was so bagged most of the time, he was lucky he didn't fall off the cliff."

11. ROCKY COOPER

"Gary Cooper's wife was a helluva shot. She held the Long Run Woman's Skeet Record. That's good."

... AND 5 SHOOTERS FROM TODAY

Stack allows: "It's interesting as a piece of memorabilia that there's a difference in taste and style today by comparison to then. Not as many shoot anymore. It's just not as 'in' as it used to be."

1. JOHN MILIUS

"The director-screenwriter. He could be world class if he'd only work at it. I'm trying to talk him into going to the Olympic tryouts."

2. STEVEN SPIELBERG

"He directed *Jaws* (1975) and *1941* (1979). He's a good shot and getting better. I'm teaching him duck hunting."

3. ROBERT WAGNER

"I taught him to shoot. He shoots sporadically, but he's a gifted athlete."

4. JACKIE COOPER

"Another good shot."

5. JOHN RUSSELL

"I haven't seen John in a while, but he's a heavy enthusiast."

12 STAR QUOTES ABOUT LOVE AND MARRIAGE

1. WARREN BEATTY

"Marriage is a lie. How can you stand up and vow you'll stay together for life, when all the time you know you'll only stick it out while it's good?"

2. BRIGITTE BARDOT

"In my experience, which is extensive, I say you can never count on a man. . . . I hate breaking off relations and always let the man take the initiative. Afterwards, I never see my husbands or lovers again. I have nothing to say to them."

3. W. C. FIELDS

"Women are like elephants to me. I like to look at them, but I wouldn't want to own one."

4. BRITT EKLAND

"I have always been discriminating in my choice of lovers, but once in bed, I am like a slave."

5. JIM BACKUS

"Many a man owes his success to his first wife, and his second wife to his success."

6. LIV ULLMANN

"In the beginning I am easy to love. That's because I am willing to give up, or to do, anything because I am so happy with the new relationship. But since I can't get away from having been an independent woman and free spirit all my life, there comes a time when I am less easy."

7. MICKEY ROONEY

"I'm the only guy I know who has a marriage license made out to whom it may concern."

8. DORIS DAY

"I always thought God meant for us to be in twos, like the animals in the ark."

9. LEE MAJORS

"It really wasn't my fault [the breakup of his marriage to Farrah Fawcett]. It was the gremlin's. It makes me have another drink when I shouldn't, stay out a little later than I should, maybe not call when I should have. Y'see, there's a little gremlin in all of us. I just happen to have more than most."

10. RICHARD BURTON

"I've never understood women. I've no idea what's going on in their minds. They have such strange circuitous ways. I'm easily manipulated by them."

11. MARILYN MONROE

"I have too many fantasies to be a housewife."

12. ZSA ZSA GABOR

"A girl must marry for love—and keep on marrying until she finds it."

MICHAEL LEVINE'S 10 MOST SOUGHT-AFTER ADDRESSES OF MOVIE STARS

Michael Levine, twenty-six, decided in 1976 to turn his ten-year-long hobby of collecting autographs into something commercial. The result was a sort of *Guinness Book* of addresses: *How To Reach Anyone*

Bo Derek, the first cinema sex symbol of the 1980s who shot to international fame in *10* (1980), is the star most people want to write to.

Who's Anyone (Price/Stern/Sloan, $4.95). It contains some 3,200 addresses for people such as Woody Allen and Alcoholics Anonymous general manager Robert Pearson to Mae West and former Nixon Press Secretary Ronald Ziegler.

Says Levine: "The top mail-getter currently seems to be Bo Derek. I understand she receives some 50,000 pieces a week at 1888 Century Park East, Suite 1400, Los Angeles, CA."

1. BO DEREK
2. BARBRA STREISAND
3. JOHN TRAVOLTA
4. ROBERT REDFORD
5. JANE FONDA
6. AL PACINO
7. WOODY ALLEN
8. MERYL STREEP
9. MAE WEST
10. DARTH VADER from *Star Wars* (1977)

Their addresses, along with 3,190 more, can be found in Levine's book. He's already working on a revised edition. Levine: "We hope to have out an up-to-date edition annually because most of these celebrities are highly mobile and constantly change their residences. It's a constant updating process. Six months from now, there'll be a new Bo Derek, and, of course, we'll want her in our book, too."

3 HOLLYWOOD COUPLES WHO MARRIED EACH OTHER TWICE

1. RICHARD BURTON and ELIZABETH TAYLOR
   They were first married in 1964 following their tempestuous affair during

Elizabeth Taylor and Richard Burton, illustrating their stormy marriage, are a Hollywood rarity in that they have married each other twice.

the filming of *Cleopatra* (1963), each of them shedding his respective mate to do so. After a ten-year stormy marriage, they divorced in 1974. They realized later that they couldn't live without each other, so they remarried in 1975. And, having finally realized that they *really* couldn't live with each other either, they divorced a second time in 1976.

2. ROBERT WAGNER and NATALIE WOOD
   In what seemed to be one of those ideal Hollywood marriages, these two young, popular film stars got married in 1957. They appeared to have everything going for them, but wedded bliss lasted only until 1963, by which time their separate careers had driven them apart. Both married again and got divorced. Then in 1972, in a sort of nostalgic Harlequin tale of true love, they were remarried. They make such a beautiful couple, they just have to make it this time.

3. EFREM ZIMBALIST, JR., and LORANDA SPAULING
   Zimbalist, a man who takes his commitments seriously and is not frivolous in making them, married Loranda in 1956, six years after he was widowed by his first wife. After a thirteen-year marriage, he and Loranda divorced, lived apart for three years, decided that the divorce was a mistake and remarried in 1972. The course of true love never runs smoothly, or so the saying goes.

10 MOVIE STARS REVEAL HOW THEY EXERCISE AND KEEP FIT

1. MARTIN SHEEN
   "I've altered my lifestyle a great deal since my heart attack while filming *Apocalypse Now* (1979). I do a lot of running now, take handfuls of vitamins—around sixty a day—and watch my diet. No cakes or sweets. What I really miss now is smoking cigarettes. I used to be a four-packs-a-day man. Never smoked a cigarette I didn't enjoy. I've also given up booze."

2. CHRISTOPHER REEVE
   "While I was in London filming *Superman II,* I'd work out every day in a gym on a strict weight-lifting program. Normally, I play volleyball and tennis whenever and wherever I am."

3. JANE FONDA
   "My daily workouts combine aerobic dance, running, and stretching exercises into an all-purpose body-aching program. Hard workouts lasting up to two hours make the heart and lungs really work, get blood oxygenated and circulating, and limber up the body. You have to keep going until it hurts. The benefit is in going beyond the pain. That's how I not only keep fit, but have the physical and mental energy necessary to confront daily programs without getting depressed or irritable."

4. JILL CLAYBURGH

"I try to jog at least five miles a day, early in the morning."

5. MICHAEL DOUGLAS

"I run seven miles a day, seven days a week. If I'm working on a movie, I run after work. Otherwise, I like to start the day with a long workout."

6. JACQUELINE BISSET

"I call my program 'organic exercise.' Whatever I'm doing—walking, swimming, or just puttering around the house—I put as much energy into as possible. By taking an interest in everything I do, I'm always in good shape."

7. VALERIE PERRINE

"I have a basic contour routine I go through several times a week. It starts with stretching, push-ups, and sit-ups, and gradually incorporates more strenuous exercises. For fun and fitness, though, I love tennis."

8. BRITT EKLAND

"I roller-skate at Flipper's in Hollywood every night, attend a fitness class three times a week for an hour and a half, and work out on Nautilus equipment once a week. I'm also very careful to eat right."

9. JILL IRELAND

"Horseback riding is invigorating, challenging, and strenuous. It's the best way I know to keep fit."

10. DYAN CANNON

"Every morning, I run a few miles on the beach at Malibu, with the surf lapping at my feet. Back home, I do twenty minutes of calisthenics. And through the day, I drink lots and lots of parsley juice."

RICHARD LAMPARSKI'S 10 MOST ASKED-ABOUT MOVIE STARS OF THE PAST

Drawing upon his background of public relations for Paramount Television, CBS Radio, the Ice Capades, and as Associate Producer for a series of NBC-TV pilot films, Richard Lamparski, in the mid-1960s, created a successful New York-based radio series entitled "Whatever Became of . . . ?" Everyone, it seemed, was interested in knowing what happened to his favorite celebrities after they faded from the public eye. The immense popularity of his radio show spawned a series of fascinating *Whatever Became of . . . ?* books, revealing the whereabouts of hundreds of stellar personalities from years gone by, with wonderful photos of then and now.

Lamparski says: "In the mail I get and on the dozens of phone-in talk shows I do here, in Canada, and in Australia, certain names keep popping up. These are the people I am asked about most often."

Turhan Bey, star of *Ali Baba and the Forty Thieves* (1943), here shown with Jon Hall and Andy Devine, is now a photographer in Vienna.

1. DEANNA DURBIN
   She won instant fame as a singing teenage star in her first picture, *Three Smart Girls* (1936), and remained a top box-office draw for a decade. "She is and has been, for all the fourteen years I've been doing this work, the number one celebrity I am asked about."
2. The OUR GANG and LITTLE RASCALS cast members.
3. TURHAN BEY
   He was a dapper Turkish leading man who had a good run in Hollywood during World War II, when the more established stars were away in military service. His big films: *Arabian Nights* (1942); *Ali Baba and the Forty Thieves* (1943); *Dragon Seed* (1944).
4. GLORIA JEAN
   The former child singing star who debuted in 1939 at age eleven in *The Underpup,* and was a second-feature rival to Deanna Durbin.
5. JUNE PREISSER
   A 1940s Universal blonde comedy featured player.
6. LON McALLISTER
   A leading man in the late '30s and '40s.
7. VERA-ELLEN
   The diminutive musical comedy star of the '40s and early '50s. Her big films: *The Kid From Brooklyn* (1946); *On the Town* (1949); *White Christmas* (1954).

8. MARGARET LINDSAY
   Leading lady of the '30s and '40s.
9. THE THREE STOOGES
   Moe Howard, Curly Howard, and Larry Fine.
10. JAMES CAGNEY
    Leading man, whose gangster pictures made him a top draw in the '30s and '40s. "He's the most asked-about superstar of yesteryear."

... AND WHATEVER BECAME OF THE ABOVE-LISTED STARS

1. DEANNA DURBIN lives in Paris, retired, and is a grandmother.
2. With the exception of TOMMY BOND ("Butch"), who is a TV station executive in Fresno, California, all the OUR GANG cast members are no longer connected with the entertainment industry, or are deceased.
3. TURHAN BEY is a photographer in Vienna.
4. GLORIA JEAN works for Redkin Cosmetics, lives in the San Fernando Valley, California, and has a child.
5. JUNE PREISSER lives in Pompano Beach, Florida, and is widowed.
6. LON McALLISTER owns and manages tourist cabins in northern California.
7. VERA-ELLEN continues to study dance, her lifelong love, and lives in Hollywood.
8. MARGARET LINDSAY lives in West Hollywood, is still available for work, and occasionally does small parts.
9. THE THREE STOOGES have all passed away.
10. CAGNEY, who lives most of the year on Martha's Vineyard, did a feature role in a 1980 movie.

PSYCHIC KEBRINA KINKADE'S "PAST LIVES OF 6 STARS"

In searching for the truth about reincarnation, leading West Coast psychic Kebrina Kinkade has focused her work on celebrities. In a quiet, dark room, the psychic managed to regress each of six well-known subjects through the subconscious mind to a former life. the results of these experiments are in her new book, *Past Lives of the Stars*.

1. SEAN CONNERY
   In the 1860s he'd given up a life of luxury in England to build a railroad through Africa. He stayed to live with two black women, each of whom bore him sons. He died from drinking too much liquor.

2. GEORGE HAMILTON

   In the 1880s he was a ruthless rubber plantation owner in South America. He was obsessed with power and money, and lots of women. Many women were imported from Europe as showpieces in an opera house he financed, as well as to service him. In an unguarded moment, a field worker shot him to death. Just goes to show you that even a hundred years ago, good help was hard to find.

3. MAC DAVIS

   In the early 1920s, he was a Mexican bandit in a zoot suit, who shot dice, hustled, stole, and did anything to get by. (Sounds like the music business, doesn't it?) After getting caught, he spent time in jail, where the toilet was a hole in the ground, everything smelled like urine, and the food was full of flies and maggots. Some things, like Mexican jails, never change; but the experience was enough to make him go straight.

4. LEE MAJORS

   Left orphaned in France in the early 1800s, he set sail for America, where he settled to raise a family. During the Civil War, he was a Union Army officer. Whereas the other subjects were able to see their deaths, Majors wasn't. "I can't see anymore. I just don't want to talk about it. It's blocked. I just can't face death."

5. PHYLLIS DILLER

   She was the daughter of a potato farmer in Germany in the mid-1600s. She married a teacher and choirmaster, and had seven children. She raised vegetables and was a great housekeeper; well, maybe some things do change.

6. LOLA FALANA

   In the nineteenth century, believe it or not, as Ripley would say, she was a white man, who was married to a very pretty and very evil young lady who killed their little girl. It broke his heart. Lola Falana a white man? What a waste!

6

CHAPTER

A STAR IS BORN

Or: *Breaking and Entering the Film Business . . . Or Is It the Fad Business?*

ROGER CORMAN'S LIST OF 11 IMPORTANT CELEBRITIES TO WHOM HE GAVE THEIR FIRST BREAKS IN THE FILM BUSINESS

Producer/director Roger Corman was the creative force behind American International Pictures for almost two decades before forming his own company, Crown International Pictures. Most of his nearly 200 movies (51 of which he directed) were shot in a matter of days, sometimes hours, on a skin-tight budget, and more often than not their titles were outrageously lurid: *Naked Paradise* (1957), *The She-Gods of Shark Reef* (1958), *A Bucket of Blood* (1959), and *Bloody Mama* (1970). His subject matter was always exploitation: bikers, gangsters, drugs, horror, and creature features. His greatest acclaim came for his series of Edgar Allen Poe adaptations, but they too were typical Corman productions. For example, *The Raven* (1963), his most admired horror satire, derived from Poe, was shot in three days because he had a moody old set that he didn't want to see go to waste.

Along the way, Corman has nurtured more future artists of film than any other producer in the industry, except perhaps for Walt Disney. "I think it's a worthwhile thing," says Corman, "to help a young person with talent to get his start in films. It's enjoyable and stimulating and I have generally made money at it."

1. FRANCIS FORD COPPOLA
   After serving as Corman's assistant, Coppola was given his first picture to direct, *Dementia* (1963). He has since proven his mettle with such pictures as *The Godfather* (1972), *The Godfather: Part II* (1974), and *Apocalypse Now* (1979).

2. PETER BOGDANOVICH
   His first film was *Targets* (1968), which led directly to *The Last Picture Show* (1971), *What's Up, Doc?* (1972), and *Paper Moon* (1973). Then, after three bombs in a row, he went back to Corman, who gave him another shot when nobody else would: *Saint Jack* (1979).

3. MARTIN SCORSESE
   After cutting his directorial teeth on *Woodstock* (1970), he got his first solo dramatic assignment from Corman, *Boxcar Bertha* (1972). He's since gone on to *Alice Doesn't Live Here Anymore* (1974), *Taxi Driver* (1976), and *Raging Bull* (1980).

4. CHARLES BRONSON
   Although Bronson had been doing small parts in films for six years, Corman gave him his first starring role as *Machine Gun Kelly* (1957). His career really started with that picture.

5. JACK NICHOLSON
   He gave Nicholson his first role, that of a desperate teenager holding hostages in *Cry Baby Killer* (1958); then continued to use him in *The Little Shop of Horrors* (1960), *The Raven* (1963), and others, until making him a recognizable actor of considerable talent in *Easy Rider* (1969). Nicholson went on to win an Oscar for *One Flew Over the Cuckoo's Nest* (1976).

6. ROBERT DE NIRO
   Corman gave De Niro his first part of substance as one of Ma Barker's brood in *Bloody Mama* (1970). Four years later, he became a star in *The Godfather: Part II,* written and directed by Coppola, another Corman graduate.

7. BRUCE DERN
   He was a veteran of two walk-ons when Corman gave him the third lead in *Wild Angels* (1966) and then *The Trip* (1967). He went on to star in such films as *Silent Running* (1972), *Coming Home* (1978), and *Middle-Age Crazy* (1980).

8. PETER FONDA
   Though Fonda had already done several movie leads, it was Corman's *Wild Angels* (1966) that started his rebel image; and three years later, with *Easy Rider,* Corman gave Fonda his first shot at producing. They did many films together.

Charles Bronson, to whom Roger Corman gave his first starring role, here strikes his best Jordache Jeans pose with Richard Burton in *The Sandpiper* (1965).

9. ROBERT TOWNE

Corman discovered him and produced and directed his first screenplay, "The Last Woman on Earth" (1960). Fourteen years later, Towne won an Oscar for Best Story and Screenplay for *Chinatown* (1974), which starred Jack Nicholson.

10. MICHAEL LANDON

His first film was *I Was a Teenage Werewolf* (1957), just two years before he became a star on TV's "Bonanza."

11. ROBERT VAUGHN

Vaughn burst into films as Corman's *Teenage Caveman* (1958), and went on to become a national hero as TV's "Man from U.N.C.L.E." (1964–68).

JIM MURRAY'S LIST OF 6 ATHLETES WHO'VE BECOME REPUTABLE ACTORS

States Murray: "I'm not sure I understand this, but it seems that more football players make the crossover into acting, and more of them are successful than from any other sport."

1. ALEX KARRAS

"Former football pro, has done some real nice work. Surprisingly good. I especially liked him in *Babe* (1975)—that TV movie with Susan Clark about the life of Babe Didrickson."

2. O. J. SIMPSON

"An outstanding football player. He's made some good TV commercials, and in the things I've seen him in, like *The Towering Inferno* (1974), he was believable."

3. CHUCK CONNORS

"Pretty good in that 'Rifleman' (1958–63) series. But he's not so much a baseball player turned actor. I think he was an actor who played professional ball. Even then he was acting."

4. MERLIN OLSEN

"Here's another football player who's done well. He plays a continuing role in 'Little House on the Prairie' (1974–present) and does a damn nice job."

5. DON MEREDITH

"I've never really seen him, but I hear he's good."

6. JOHNNY WEISSMULLER

"If you want to go back a few years. Now, Johnny wasn't what you'd call Shakespearean or anything, but for what he had to work with, he did a credible job."

... AND A LIST OF 6 ACTORS WHO
WERE BETTER ATHLETES

1. MAX BAER
   "A pretty good fighter, but a lousy actor."
2. BABE RUTH
   "He tried it too, but wasn't too good."
3. JIM BROWN
   "He never should've been an actor."
4. MIKE HENRY
   "He was a Tarzan, and I'm beyond my Tarzan days."
5. JOE NAMATH
   "I like Joe, and he's done okay, but an actor he ain't. But he sure can sell panty hose and cologne."
6. MUHAMMAD ALI
   "I've never seen him in anything, but I suspect that he shouldn't be acting, and that's why I never bothered."

20 FAMOUS STARS AND THEIR REAL NAMES

When Vera Miles came to Hollywood from Kansas in 1948, she found it somewhat unsettling that she wouldn't be able to use her real name in her film career. It wasn't that her name was awkward or clumsy but that somebody in the movie business was already using it. Vera Miles, who was born Vera Ralston, had to change her given name because Vera Hruba Ralston was Queen of Republic Studios. Within the year of her arrival, Vera met and married Bob Miles, and it was under her married name that she pursued her career.

For Stewart Granger, it was a similar experience. He was perfectly happy with his real name, and though everyone agreed that it was as good a name as you can get, it still had to be changed. Why? It just wouldn't do to have *two* James Stewarts in the movies.

These two stars are unusual in their situations. Generally, name changes were done at the discretion of the major film studios in their "star buildup," which was designed to create—or rather manufacture—a personality suitable for the movies. Consequently, most of the early stars of Hollywood emerged celebrities under different names than those with which they were born.

Louis B. Mayer, MGM czar and movie mogul said: "I'll tell you what's in a name. Would a rose be as sweet if it were called a potato? Obviously not. Same goes for stars. If a name has more than two syllables, forget it. Nobody out there in the great unwashed is going to identify with a name like Frederick Austerlitz. It sounds German, and German's a dirty word. But Fred Astaire—now, there's a name that will look good on a marquee."

Changing an actor's name was also a psychological lever for the big studios. It showed their power to control the lives of the actors they had under contract, a power they exercised to the fullest.

Here are twenty wonderful original names of actors, and who they became in their climb to stardom:

1. Margarita Cansino: RITA HAYWORTH
2. Archibald Leach: CARY GRANT
3. Richard Jenkins, Jr.: RICHARD BURTON
4. Lucille LeSueur: JOAN CRAWFORD

Before she became Rita Hayworth, Margarita Cansino broke into pictures with Gary Leon as a dance team in *Dante's Inferno* (1935).

5. Lily Chauchoin: CLAUDETTE COLBERT
6. Ramon Esteves: MARTIN SHEEN
7. Edna Rae Gilhooly: ELLEN BURSTYN
8. Harlean Carpentier: JEAN HARLOW
9. William Ingle-Finch: PETER FINCH
10. Julius Garfinkle: JOHN GARFIELD
11. Emmanuel Goldenberg: EDWARD G. ROBINSON
12. Shirley Schrift: SHELLEY WINTERS
13. Ruby Stevens: BARBARA STANWYCK
14. Issur Danielovitch: KIRK DOUGLAS
15. Marion Morrison: JOHN WAYNE
16. William Henry Pratt: BORIS KARLOFF
17. Leonard Slye: ROY ROGERS
18. Natasha Gurdin: NATALIE WOOD
19. Frances Gumm: JUDY GARLAND
20. Gerald Silberman: GENE WILDER

8 ACTORS WHOSE FEATURES WERE USED IN THE COMPOSITE FOR THE UNKNOWN SOUGHT AS THE LEAD IN COLUMBIA'S *GOLDEN BOY*

The talent search was not quite the big ballyhoo given the massive hunt for Scarlett O'Hara and Rhett Butler for MGM's *Gone With the Wind,* but Columbia Studios did its best to find a new young actor for their upcoming big picture, *Golden Boy* (1939). They created a composite of eight established stars as a sort of guide to help them find exactly the right new face.

To portray the role of the violinist who sought fame and glory as a boxer in Clifford Odets' play, "Golden Boy," the casting office wanted an unknown who had the following facial attributes:

1. Tyrone Power's hair
2. Errol Flynn's forehead
3. Charles Boyer's eyes
4. Wayne Morris' nose
5. Cary Grant's chin
6. Joel McCrea's jaw contour
7. Robert Taylor's mouth
8. Franchot Tone's smile

Guess who finally fit the bill? WILLIAM HOLDEN. The picture made him a star.

The *Golden Boy* talent hunt in 1939 was crystalized in this composite photo for which Columbia Studios artists combined the features of eight well-known actors.

William Holden's was the face chosen as the closest to the elusive ideal sought for the *Golden Boy* lead. Here, he shows how he got the part to costars Adolph Menjou and Barbara Stanwyck.

EILEEN FORD'S LIST OF 6 OF HER TOP MODELS TO BECOME FILM STARS

Eileen Ford, founder and president of Ford Models, Inc., the top modeling agency in the country, has groomed many unknowns into celebrity models. Sometimes her models make the leap from modeling to motion pictures.

1. LAUREN HUTTON
   "A worker, a friend, who deserves her success."
2. JANE FONDA
   "But she has forgotten me."
3. CANDICE BERGEN
   "She never forgets."
4. MAUDE ADAMS
   "Who will get there soon."
5. ALI MacGRAW
   "A creative and loving human being."
6. BROOKE SHIELDS
   "It is nice to be fifteen! And the best is yet to come."

20 FADS AND FASHIONS SPARKED BY MOVIE STARS

Are we really *A Nation of Sheep* as culture-observer and author Vance Packard would have us believe? We might argue the point, but all the evidence that Mr. Packard needs can be found in the multitude of fads and fashions that were started by film stars and which the American public, like so many sheep, has clutched to its collective bosom.

1. MAE MURRAY
   In the 1920s, Mae Murray's bee-stung lips, which were actually an exaggerated heart shape, were imitated by other glamour queens of the screen as well as by the flapper generation at large.
2. JEAN HARLOW
   When she burst upon the screen scene in the early 1930s, platinum blondes came into vogue overnight. Blonde, almost blinding blonde, became sexy. Harlow bleached her hair so often that, rumors had it, her untimely death was actually the result of brain damage from peroxide poisoning.
   Harlow also popularized the exaggerated penciled-arch eyebrows but in order to draw them in, girls had to first shave their natural eyebrows. Lana Turner's were shaved during this period when she was just beginning in the film business, and her eyebrows never grew back.

The original blonde sex symbol, Jean Harlow, showed that blondes can have more fun. Thousands of women ran out and bleached their hair to find out first-hand.

3. MARLENE DIETRICH

When she arrived in Hollywood in the early 1930s, she kicked off a fashion style that women everywhere copied: She wore slacks and men's-style jackets.

4. JOAN CRAWFORD

As Sadie Thompson in *Rain* (1932), Crawford replaced bee-stung lips with a drastically overdrawn mouth. Millions followed suit, often with comic results, as exaggerated liplines wandered from nose to chin.

5. CLAUDETTE COLBERT

The following year, hair-wizard Perc Westmore created Claudette Colbert's perky bangs, which hit mid-forehead. Not every woman in America ran out to copy the look, but enough did to make it appear that a bang-plague was upon us.

6. CLARK GABLE

When Gable removed his shirt in *It Happened One Night* (1934) and revealed a bare chest, every man in America burned his T-shirt in what was perhaps the first men's liberation movement.

7. BING CROSBY

With his casual, relaxed attire, he set a new fashion trend for men sans neckties and sports jackets, kicking off some more men's liberation.

8. KATHARINE HEPBURN

As the ultimate liberated woman of the 1940s screen, Kate Hepburn newly popularized pants for women, and made them acceptable everyday wear.

9. INGRID BERGMAN

In *Intermezzo* (1939), her first American film, Bergman, who refused to shave her eyebrows, started the initial wave toward natural makeup. The natural look was still a long way off, but the eyebrows were a good start.

10. JANE RUSSELL

The only thing that the flat oater *The Outlaw* (1941) had going for it was the double-barreled, opulent chest of Jane Russell. In a single stroke, she not only made massive mammaries fashionable and sexy, but she became an international star two years before the picture was released. It was hard for all ladies to affect the Jane Russell look, but her arrival on the scene heralded the last toll for the curveless boyish vogue started in the flapper era.

11. LESLIE CARON

Hand-picked by Gene Kelly as his dancing partner in *An American in Paris* (1951), French actress/dancer Caron impressed American ladies with her gamine hair cut, and the waif look took off. It was as unattractive as it was popular. And fortunately it died out, but was resurrected by Mia Farrow in the late 1960s.

12. GINA LOLLOBRIGIDA

Her poodle cut in *Trapeze* (1956) inspired football fields full of high school girls to trade in their pony tails and page boys for the new imported Italian look.

13. JAMES DEAN

    And while girls were going poodle, the guys were all sporting the uniform of the day: jeans, T-shirt, and windbreaker, as popularized by James Dean in *Rebel Without a Cause* (1956).

14. ESTHER WILLIAMS

    Who says that swim wear has to be functional? Not Esther Williams, who kicked off poolside fashions in the mid-1950s that were more to be looked at than to swim in.

15. ELIZABETH TAYLOR

    With *Cleopatra* (1963), Liz Taylor popularized the heavily lined eye makeup and pearlized lipstick look. If as many people who followed the fashion had gone to see the movie, it would have been a huge success, instead of the bomb that it was.

16. AUDREY HEPBURN

    One of the more lasting fashion trends was initiated by Audrey Hepburn in *Breakfast at Tiffany's* (1961), in which her hair had blond streaks. Women are still doing it.

Leading man Robert Redford got the part of Sundance in *Butch Cassidy and the Sundance Kid* (1969) when Steve McQueen couldn't do it. He became a superstar, and inspired millions around the world to grow imitations of his sexy mustache. Redford, soon thereafter, shaved his off.

17. AUDREY HEPBURN

Her oversized sunglasses in several pictures, but most notably in *Two for the Road* (1967), became the jetsetters' classic, and were adopted by another international trendsetter, Jackie Kennedy.

18. ROBERT REDFORD

When he costarred with Paul Newman in *Butch Cassidy and the Sundance Kid* (1969), Redford became the first contemporary superstar with a mustache, and hundreds of thousands of young men around the world stopped shaving their upper lips in an effort to cash in on the new sex symbol's sex appeal.

19. DIANE KEATON

Her makeshift mix of men's and women's clothes in *Annie Hall* (1977), using vests, floppy pants, floppy hats, shirts and ties, floppy glasses, and floppy hair, caught the imagination of both the under- and over-twenty sets.

20. JOHN TRAVOLTA

In addition to igniting an international disco fever (which was already well under way, but he certainly gave it a huge boost) with *Saturday Night Fever* (1978), he also gave white suits with black shirts a whole new fad-life.

KEITH LARSEN'S LIST OF 10 ACTORS WHO ARE EQUALLY TALENTED ON THE OTHER SIDE OF THE CAMERA AS DIRECTORS

Under personal contract to Walter Mirisch, Keith Larsen debuted in films with *The Rose Bowl Story* (1952) and went on to become a leading man in a string of pictures like *The Son of Belle Starr* (1953), *Wichita* (1955), and *Fury River* (1961). Simultaneously, he built a substantial reputation in television as the star of four series: "The Hunter" (1954–55), "Brave Eagle" (1955–56), "Northwest Passage" (1958–59), and "Aquanauts" (1960–61). Since the mid-1960s, he's concentrated on directing as well as acting with such films as *Mission Batangas* (1969), *Night of the Witches* (1970), *Run to Cougar Mountain* (1972), and *White Water* (1976).

Says Larsen: "I first became interested in directing in the early fifties and cut my teeth on television, as I was able to promote directing a lot of the episodes of my series. What appeals to me about directing as opposed to acting is that you have more creative control, and more opportunity to express your imagination. It's more exciting and greatly satisfying.

"Here are ten actors who have gotten into directing and done a damn good job. They're in no particular order."

1. ALAN ARKIN
2. JACK LEMMON
3. ORSON WELLES
4. PETER USTINOV
5. CARL REINER

6. ROBERT MONTGOMERY
7. PAUL NEWMAN
8. ROBERT REDFORD
9. GENE KELLY
10. JACK NICHOLSON

... AND 2 DIRECTORS WHO HAVE MADE NEW CAREERS AS ACTORS

1. JOHN HUSTON

2. JOHN HOUSEMAN

DENNIS WEAVER'S LIST OF 9 MOVIE ACTORS WHO HAVE BEEN BITTEN BY THE SINGING BUG

"In each of us, I think, there's a secret desire to be something in addition to what we are," says Dennis Weaver, of TV's "Gunsmoke" (1955–62) and "McCloud" (1970–77) fame. Weaver's secret leanings were fulfilled when he recently cut an album of some favorite tunes, called "The World Needs Country Music." And he's not the only actor to be smitten with singing:

1. CLINT EASTWOOD
   He recorded "Barroom Buddies" with pal Merle Haggard as part of the soundtrack for *Bronco Billy* (1980). "And I'll be darned if the thing didn't get into the Top 10 Country charts. And the only thing I have to say about that is, 'Clint, if you're gonna sing with Merle Haggard, you're bound to have a number one hit.' But it's a bit like playing with a stacked deck."
2. BURT REYNOLDS
   He sings "Let's Do Something Cheap and Superficial" in *Smokey and the Bandit II* (1980). "Maybe you won't remember this, but Burt tried singing before, a few years ago when he was a twosome with Dinah Shore. And if you listen to his record real close, you might recognize the female backup singer doing the harmony."
3. SISSY SPACEK
   Has recorded a whole album in her role of Loretta Lynn, the *Coalminer's Daughter* (1980).
4. GARY BUSEY
   Recorded a whole album of early rock tunes for *The Buddy Holly Story* (1979).
5. DYAN CANNON

She sings two songs, "Two Sides to Every Story" and a duet with Willie Nelson, "Uncloudy Day," in *Honeysuckle Rose* (1980).

6. KAREN BLACK

She not only sang in *Nashville* (1975) but wrote her own songs as well.

7. RICHARD HARRIS

Has had a best-selling album called "MacArthur Park" with songs written by Jimmy Webb, and followed it with a second album called "His Greatest Performances."

8. ALBERT FINNEY

He entered the recording sweepstakes with "Albert Finney's Album."

9. CYBIL SHEPPARD

She did it, too, with "Cybil Does It . . . to Cole Porter."

DENNIS WEAVER'S LIST OF 16 SINGERS WHO'VE SUCCESSFULLY CROSSED THE ARTISTIC LINES TO BECOME SUCCESSFUL ACTORS

Weaver claims: "It's true that a lot of actors like to try their hand at singing. I think it's only natural. But the reverse side of the coin is also true. A lot of singers get the acting bug. Yet, traditionally, it seems to me, singers are more easily accepted as actors, on the whole, whereas there seems to be a built-in prejudice against actors cutting a few records, almost as if they're invading a territory that doesn't belong to them. But when a singer comes into acting, sometimes you find some wonderful actors. And you just start with Bing Crosby . . ."

1. BING CROSBY

The star crooner and band singer got into pictures in the 1930s and went on to win an Academy Award for *Going My Way* (1944).

2. JEANETTE MACDONALD

She was a concert singer and NELSON EDDY was an opera star, but together they were movie magic, and made such unforgettable musicals as *Naughty Marietta* (1935), *Rose Marie* (1936), and *The Girl of the Golden West* (1938).

3. FRANK SINATRA

He was a crooner and band vocalist, and a teenage rave in the 1940s. He made his picture bow in musicals, but went on to win an Oscar for a dramatic performance in *From Here to Eternity* (1953). One of his all-time classic films, *High Society* (1956), was with fellow crooner Bing Crosby.

4. ELVIS PRESLEY

The king of rock and roll turned to movies in 1956 with *Love Me*

Tender, and stayed on in Hollywood to make thirty-two films, all of which made money. He'd still be cranking them out if not for his untimely death.

Bing Crosby, here with Bob Hope and Dorothy Lamour in *The Road to Utopia* (1945), has been the most successful singer-turned-actor in the history of films.

5. BARBRA STREISAND

   What a voice! And she won an Oscar in her first picture, *Funny Girl* (1968). And today, she's one of the biggest stars in the world.

6. DIANA ROSS

   She used to be the lead singer of the Supremes pop group, and was nominated for an Oscar for her film debut as Billie Holiday in *Lady Sings the Blues* (1972).

7. BETTE MIDLER

   More recently, she did the same thing. Her first picture, *The Rose* (1979), garnered an Oscar nomination for her.

8. KRIS KRISTOFFERSON

   The popular folk and country singer who's written some classic country tunes like "Help Me Make It Through the Night" turned to acting in 1972. He's made some dandy pictures, too, like *A Star Is Born* (1976), with Streisand, and *Semi-Tough* (1979), with Burt Reynolds.

9. MAC DAVIS

   Costarred with Nick Nolte in *North Dallas Forty* (1979), got great reviews, and is off to a fine start.

10. JOHN DENVER

    He made his film debut in the highly successful *Oh, God!* (1977), "but his first acting job was on 'McCloud.'"

11. OLIVIA NEWTON-JOHN

    Made her film debut in one of the biggest money-making blockbusters of all time, *Grease* (1978).

12. DOLLY PARTON

    Her first film, *Nine to Five* (1980), was followed by her teaming with Burt Reynolds for *The Best Little Whorehouse in Texas* (1981).

13. WILLIE NELSON

    Debuted in *Electric Horseman* (1980) with Jane Fonda and Robert Redford, then went immediately into his first starring vehicle, *Honeysuckle Rose* (1980).

14. JERRY REED

    Another country singer who's paired up with Burt Reynolds on a handful of films, like *Gator* (1976), *W. W. and the Dixie Dancekings* (1975), *Smokey and the Bandit* (1977), and *Smokey and the Bandit II* (1980).

15. HOYT AXTON

    He turned in a beautiful performance in *The Black Stallion* (1979), but he got his first acting job on 'McCloud.'

16. PAUL WILLIAMS

    He got started on TV in a "Baretta" and went on to co-star with Burt Reynolds in the *Smokey* pictures.

Concludes Weaver: "You know, I could probably trot out some others if I thought about it some more, but I think you see my point. It's just easier to go from singing to acting than the other way around."

7 THE AWFUL TRUTH

CHAPTER

Or *Sometimes the Truth Hurts*

DR. LAURENCE J. PETER'S LIST OF 13 WHO ACHIEVED THEIR LEVEL OF COMPETENCE AND WENT BEYOND TO ACHIEVE THEIR PETER PRINCIPLE

While a professor of education at the University of Southern California, Dr. Laurence J. Peter discovered a universal truth. He noticed competent educators being promoted, and becoming incompetent administrators. His research led to *The Peter Principle,* a best-selling book which remained on the *New York Times* best-seller list for over a year and has since been translated into thirty-seven languages. It has led to four additional volumes: *The Peter Prescription, The Peter Plan, Peter Quotations,* and *The Peter People.*

States Peter: "Basically, the Peter principle says that in every hierarchy an individual tends to rise to his level of incompetence. Or, in other words, the cream rises until it sours."

Here, then, are some high-profile cinematic examples:

1. RONALD REAGAN
2. MARLON BRANDO
3. GEORGE C. SCOTT
4. ROBERT ALTMAN
5. SYLVESTER STALLONE
6. JERRY LEWIS
7. MARGAUX HEMINGWAY
8. JOHN TRAVOLTA
9. SUE LYON
10. DAVID BEGELMAN
11. LINDA BLAIR
12. CAROL BAKER
13. STEVEN SPIELBERG

Ronald Reagan, whose movie career peaked with *Kings Row* (1941), which costarred Ann Sheridan, may have achieved his Peter Principle with his election as president of the United States. We certainly hope not.

... And 3 Old-Timers

1. FATTY ARBUCKLE
2. HARRY LANGDON
3. JOHN GILBERT

10 FAMOUS QUOTES ABOUT HOLLYWOOD

1. DAVID WARK GRIFFITH, film pioneer, director, producer, star-maker:
   "It's a shame to take this country away from the rattlesnakes."
2. FRED ALLEN, humorist and actor:
   "Hollywood is a place where people from Iowa mistake each other for stars."
3. WILSON MIZNER, highly quotable screenwriter:
   "You can take all the sincerity in Hollywood, put it into the navel of a fruitfly, and still have enough room for three caraway seeds and a producer's (or agent's) heart."
4. MARILYN MONROE
   "Hollywood is a place where they'll pay you fifty thousand for a kiss and fifty cents for your soul."
5. OSCAR LEVANT, pianist and insult master:
   "Strip away the phony tinsel of Hollywood and you find the real tinsel underneath."
6. DOROTHY PARKER, columnist and wit:
   "If all those sweet young things were laid end to end, I wouldn't be surprised."
7. REX REED, critic and author:
   "In Hollywood, if you don't have happiness, you send out for it."
8. ANDY WARHOL, artist and film producer:
   "I love Hollywood. Everybody's plastic. I want to be plastic."
9. JANE FONDA:
   "Working in Hollywood does give you a certain expertise in the field of prostitution."
10. FRANK CAPRA, director:
    "There is one word which aptly describes Hollywood—*nervous!*"

THE FIRST 3 MEMBERS OF THE DULL MEN'S HALL OF FAME

Now they've done it. The Carroll, Iowa, Chamber of Commerce has made it official. The town is now the home of The Dull Men's Hall of Fame. Some residents are incensed, but Chamber of Commerce manager Douglas Alexander says that it is "a dandy promotion." He's quick to add that no insult is intended. "Dull is not boring. This is not a slight on any of the Hall of Famers. It's to honor the type of man who doesn't go around jumping on every bandwagon."

The first three inductees are:

1. OZZIE NELSON (1906–75)
   Bandleader, radio and film actor, who became famous on TV's "Ozzie and Harriet" (1952–66).
2. NIGEL BRUCE (1895–1953)
   Venerable supporting actor, whose greatest fame came as the screen's most memorable Dr. Watson to Basil Rathbone's Sherlock Holmes series (1939–46).
3. ROBERT YOUNG (1907–)
   Light comedy leading man who debuted in films in 1931. After some fifty films he became hugely popular on television in "Father Knows Best" (1954–62) and "Marcus Welby, M.D." (1969–76).

MR. BLACKWELL'S 10 WORST-DRESSED WOMEN IN THE MOVIES

On the first Tuesday of every January for the past eighteen years, Hollywood fashion designer Mr. Blackwell separates the wheat from the chaff, the chic from the goats, in his annual list of the World's Ten Worst-Dressed Women. As much an institution as Groundhog Day, the tart-tongued designer zings the ladies he feels have violated fashion's prime purpose—to glorify womanhood.

1. BO DEREK (Worst-Dressed, 1979)
   "The love child of the 1980s gets a minus ten for fashion."
2. JILL CLAYBURGH (2nd Worst-Dressed, 1979)
   "She dresses like an African bush . . . waiting for her safari."
3. VALERIE PERRINE (9th Worst-Dressed, 1979)
   "She looks like the bride of Frankenstein doing the Ziegfeld Follies."
4. MARGAUX HEMINGWAY (10th Worst-Dressed, 1979)
   "A Hanukkah bush . . . the day after Christmas."
5. HELEN REDDY (2nd Worst-Dressed, 1975)
   "She doesn't know who she is. She wears see-through clothes that show her bosoms—whatever they are."
6. BETTE MIDLER (Worst-Dressed, 1973)
7. JULIE ANDREWS (2nd Worst-Dressed, 1972)
8. MIA FARROW (3rd Worst-Dressed, 1972)
9. ALI MacGRAW (Worst-Dressed, 1971)
10. SOPHIA LOREN (Worst-Dressed, 1970)

AND . . . MR. BLACKWELL'S 4 HALL-OF-FAME LIFETIME MEMBERS (WORST-DRESSED REPEAT OFFENDERS)

1. ELIZABETH TAYLOR
2. ZSA ZSA GABOR
3. BARBRA STREISAND
4. RAQUEL WELCH

BOB MICHAELSON'S LIST OF THE 6 HARDEST-TO-PHOTOGRAPH, MOST UNCOOPERATIVE FILM STARS

"It takes a lot of guts to be a successful paparazzi photographer," says Bob Michaelson. "You've got to be persistent, and bold, to get the photo you need. You've got to be willing to wait somewhere in the cold and dark to get your opportunity. And sometimes you have to physically wrestle for your equipment or film once you have your shot. Perhaps that's why there are more men in this field than women. It's physically demanding at times."

Michaelson should know. He's been at it long enough to have, at forty-five, his own agency, with a staff of twenty photographers nationwide who snap enough photos to sell over 10,000 pictures a year.

Among the movie celebrities who are often determined not to have their pictures taken are:

1. FRANK SINATRA
2. GRETA GARBO
3. BARBRA STREISAND
4. MARLON BRANDO
5. KATHARINE HEPBURN
6. WARREN BEATTY

JAMES GARNER'S 2 WORST FILMS

James Garner is a rarity in the acting game. Although essentially a television actor ("Maverick" 1957–62; "Nichols" 1971–72; "The Rockford Files" (1974–80), he has also enjoyed a highly successful film career with hits like *The Great Escape* (1963), *Grand Prix* (1966), *Support Your Local Sheriff* (1969), *The Skin Game* (1970), among others.

Garner asserts: "Everybody has their films which, after they've done, they wish they'd never done them. I've got a couple in the closet, just like everybody else."

1. *The Pink Jungle* (1968)
   Director: Delbert Mann; Garner, George Kennedy, Eva Renzi. "It was originally called *The Jolly Pink Jungle,* but fortunately, they dropped the

Barbra Streisand, dressed outrageously for *The Owl and the Pussycat* (1970) with George Segal, has been named to Mr. Blackwell's Worst-Dressed Hall of Fame.

James Garner, Eva Renzi, and George Kennedy are in hiding, possibly after the reviews came out for *The Pink Jungle* (1968).

Jolly. It was such a great picture that it was in release for about twelve minutes before it died. The director and I got into arguments about things. There was this one scene that I didn't want to do, and he insisted. So— for the scene I changed my clothes so that it wouldn't match anything we'd already shot. Of course, I thought, they won't be able to use it. . . . They used it anyway."

2. *A Man Called Sledge* (1971)

   D: Vic Morrow; Garner, Dennis Weaver, Claude Akins, John Marley. "This was one of those Italian beauties where Dino de Laurentiis promises you everything and gives you nothing."

Actually, Garner could have easily added *Health* (1980) to the list, but, professional that he is, didn't, because it was just heading into general release. However, true to his well-established m.o., director Robert Altman absolutely wasted the comedic talents of not only Garner, but Garner's costars Carol Burnett and Lauren Bacall, in a waste-of-film film about which critic Charles Champlin wrote: "It would be hard for any film to live *down* to the negative rumbles about *Health,* but *Health* is pretty ill, and there's no other way to say it."

THE FIRST ANNUAL "BEDTIME FOR BONZO" AWARDS TO 12 MAJOR STARS FOR THEIR ALL-TIME WORST MOVIES

Big-name stars are much like the rest of us. They all put their pants on one leg at a time (even Jane Fonda); they all go to the bathroom; and they all have to pay taxes (even if it is in a different bracket). They are not mini-deities, unless you can picture them with feet made of play-doh. And they make mistakes, many of which turn up on the screen, but which, alas, were best left on the farm with the other gobblers.

To the following stars we present a brass-plated statuette of a Dozing Chimpanzee in recognition of the lowest achievement of their stellar careers:

1. RAQUEL WELCH, *Myra Breckenridge* (1970)

   As bad as any movie ever made, this tasteless garbage about a sex change operation should have been sent to Sweden for some more surgery.

2. ELIZABETH TAYLOR, *Boom* (1968)

   This fuzzy Joseph Losey adaptation of a Tennessee Williams play should have been called *Plop* for the pile it resembles.

3. MARLON BRANDO, *The Missouri Breaks* (1976)

Raquel Welch gave John Huston and others an eyeful in *Myra Breckenridge* (1970), one of the worst movies ever, and the first recipient of the brass-plated Dozing Chimpanzee Award in the first annual *Bedtime for Bonzo* Award ceremonies.

This is one of those dynamite star combos (Brando and Jack Nicholson) that had as much excitement as a wet firecracker. I am an easy hook and will watch any movie, but I walked out on this one, which, incidentally, qualifies as Nicholson's worst ever as well.

4. AL PACINO, *Bobby Deerfield* (1977)
   A consummate actor in a consummate flop. We all suffered with him and co-star Marthe Keller, but only because it was such a stinker.

5. PAUL NEWMAN, *Buffalo Bill and the Indians* (1976)
   This drek was subtitled *Or Sitting Bull's History Lesson,* and should have been Newman's lesson not to work with director Robert Altman again, but he must be masochistic because he agreed to Altman's *Quintet* (1979), which has proven to be the second low point in his career.

6. BURT REYNOLDS, *Rough Cut* (1980)
   Not even Burt's abundant charm nor director Don Siegal's talent could smooth out the edges on this one, which proved rough going for an audience to sit through.

7. SYLVESTER STALLONE, *Paradise Alley* (1978)
   Stallone, who wrote, directed, and starred, never got this sappy story of three none-too-bright brothers out of Hell's Kitchen where everything got too over-done.

8. CHARLES BRONSON, *The White Buffalo* (1977)
   It should've been called *The White Elephant* or maybe *The Albino Turkey.*

9. JOHN TRAVOLTA, *Moment by Moment* (1978)
   Frame by frame, this almost wrecked his career, and gave new meaning to the word "boring."

10. GEORGE SEGAL, *The Terminal Man* (1974)
    To say the book was better is the understatement of the decade, since this picture suffered from terminal tastelessness.

11. JANE FONDA, *Comes a Horseman* (1978)
    Conceived as the ultimate Western, this film emerged as the ultimate catatonia, beautiful vistas and all.

12. ROBERT REDFORD, *The Great Gatsby* (1974)
    Sure, Francis Ford Coppola wrote the script, but—if you can believe it—the 1949 Alan Ladd version is a classic film by comparison. (This film is one of the reasons Redford now makes his own pictures.)

8 WELL-KNOWN CELEBRITIES WHO CONTRACTED CANCER DUE TO THEIR WORK ON UTAH LOCATIONS FOR HOWARD HUGHES' *THE CONQUEROR*

In the summer of 1954, 220 cast and crew members from Hollywood spent two months filming *The Conqueror* in the Utah desert near Saint George. Of that film company, an astonishingly high number—

91 people—have contracted cancer; 46 of them have died. The incident is a hotbed of controversy.

It seems painfully clear a quarter of a century after the fact that they were exposed to highly radioactive fallout from above-ground nuclear tests conducted the previous year, 137 miles away at Yucca Flat, Nevada. In grim testimony to the disastrous aftereffects of the atomic testing (which has since been banned), the small population of Saint George is plagued by an extraordinarily high rate of cancer.

The grave questions now being raised concern governmental responsibility and basic moral issues. A congressional investigative report concluded: "All evidence suggesting that radiation was having harmful effects . . . was not only disregarded but was actually suppressed." The radioactive fallout was still abundant more than a year after the testing had ceased; and the rolling dunes of Snow Canyon, where much of the filming took place, was a "hot spot" or natural reservoir for the windblown fallout. And, ironically, RKO trucks hauled 60 tons of the reddish Utah contaminated sand back to Hollywood for additional shooting.

Eight of the more illustrious members of the film company to be stricken include:

1. DICK POWELL, producer/director
   He died in 1963 from lymph cancer.
2. JOHN WAYNE, the star
   He fought a long, painful battle against lung, throat, and stomach cancer, which finally claimed him in June, 1979. One Defense Nuclear Agency scientist was reportedly quoted as saying: "Please, God, don't let us have killed John Wayne."
3. SUSAN HAYWARD, leading lady
   In the decade before she died in 1975 of a brain tumor, she suffered the ravages of skin, breast, and uterine cancer.
4. PEDRO ARMENDARIZ, costar
   He survived kidney cancer in 1960, but killed himself three years later at age 51 upon learning that he had terminal cancer of the lymphatic system.
5. AGNES MOOREHEAD, costar
   She was the first member of the company to make a connection between the fallout and the cancer risk resulting from the film. Before uterine cancer killed her in 1974, she observed: "Everybody in the picture has gotten cancer and died." And: "I should never have taken that part."
6. THOMAS GOMEZ, costar
   He died in 1971, at age 64.
7. HOWARD HUGHES, executive producer
   Unsubstantiated rumor has it that a bout with skin cancer was what drove

Susan Hayward and John Wayne are two stars who have allegedly died from cancer that was contracted during the filming of *The Conqueror* (1955), when the entire cast and crew were exposed to radioactive fallout in the Utah desert.

him to become a recluse, and to constantly wear gloves in what became known as his celebrated "germ phobia." He died in 1976, reportedly from kidney failure, which may or may not have been caused by cancer.

8. JEANNE GERSON, supporting actress

In 1965, she developed skin cancer, which was temporarily cured through surgery. Then in 1977, she contracted breast cancer, underwent a mastectomy, and began chemotherapy, which continues today. She says, "I've always been convinced that it's more than a coincidence." She initiated a class action suit against the government for gross negligence and deceit.

AND 3 CHILDREN OF THE STARS WHO VISITED THE SET OF *THE CONQUEROR* AND HAVE HAD CANCER BOUTS

1. MICHAEL WAYNE
   The eldest son of John Wayne, he developed skin cancer in 1975. He's president of Batjac Productions, which produced most of his father's later films. Says Michael: "I think my dad stayed alive on will power alone. He didn't cry over a lot of stuff that went by in the past, things that you can't do anything about. Suing the government isn't going to bring him back."
2. PATRICK WAYNE
   Michael's younger brother, forty-one, was operated on for a breast tumor; fortunately, it was not malignant.
3. TIM BARKER
   Son of Susan Hayward, Barker, thirty-five, had a benign tumor removed from his mouth in 1968. He's angry and bitter: "Will I have to go through what my mother did? . . . If the government knew that there was a possibility of exposure, why didn't they just warn us?"

That's a question being asked by a lot of people.

8 CHAPTER

STARDUST

Or: *Celebrity Selections*

BURT REYNOLDS' LIST OF THE 5 GREATEST MOVIE STUNTS

Long before he was a superstar, Burt Reynolds was a stunt actor, that is, an actor who is cast in a picture or TV show in a supporting role because he does his own stunts; it cuts down on the number of people needed on a show if someone can do his own stuntwork, so he worked regularly. As he got better parts and eventually became a bankable star, he continued—and still does—to do his own stunts (although he is not allowed by the insurance companies to take any unnecessary risks). He is a rare breed, like fellow superstar Clint Eastwood, who also prefers doing his own stuntwork. And, as you'd expect, Reynolds respects and appreciates a good stunt:

1. The high fall out of the helicopter into the air bag in *Hooper* (1978). Doubling for Reynolds, stuntman A. J. Bakunas fell 232 feet setting a new world record for a free fall onto an air mattress.
2. The car flip in *McQ* (1974) on the beach, where the car turned over seven times. It was the first time a cannon had been used to propel the rolling effect of the car. The stunt driver was Gary McCarthy.
3. The horse transfers in *Little Big Man* (1970), when Hal Needham and Alan Gibbs jumped onto the wheeler team of a six-up hooked to a stage-

Burt Reynolds is seen preparing and leaping from a helicopter in the role of *Hooper* (1978), Hollywood's number one stuntman. The actual stunt (as seen on the right) was performed by A.J. Bakunas in a 232-foot world-record-breaking free fall onto an air mattress.

coach. They then did 14-foot standing broad jumps from the back of the wheeler team to the swing team, then to the leader team, while the horses were running at a full gallop.

4. The fire gag in *Warlords of Atlantis* (1978) where five stuntmen in fire suits stood on a gasoline-soaked bridge over a moat. The fire suits were covered with rubber cement and ignited and after jumping around, the men plunged into the moat.

5. The ski stunt in *The Spy Who Loved Me* (1977), where the skier in the opening segment of the James Bond film skied off the face of the mountain and did a free fall for several thousand feet before he opened his parachute.

MARIO ANDRETTI'S LIST OF
3 CAR-RACING MOVIE CLASSICS

If there ever was a classic car-racer, it has to be Mario Andretti. Born in Montona Trieste, Italy, in 1940, he has become one of the truly great race car drivers of our time and has won hundreds of championships and awards. Most notably, he was the National Champion, U.S. Auto Club in 1965, 1966, 1969; winner of the Indianapolis 500 in 1969; and the 1979 ABC Athlete of the Year.

1. TO PLEASE A LADY (1950)
   Clark Gable, Barbara Stanwyck.

Advertising poster for *To Please a Lady* (1950), one of the best racing films of all time.

123

2. GRAND PRIX (1966)
   James Garner, Eva Marie Saint, Yves Montand.
   "The racing sequences were spectacular."
3. BULLITT (1968)
   Steve McQueen, Robert Vaughn, Jacqueline Bisset.
   "This wasn't a racing picture as such, but the car chase is the screen's all-time best."

GEORGE KENNEDY'S LIST OF 9 MEMORABLE DISASTER MOVIES

George Kennedy, who debuted in *The Little Shepherd of Kingdom Come* (1960), worked his way through featured and villainous roles to star status with *Cool Hand Luke,* for which his performance won him an Academy Award as Best Supporting Actor. His recent work has been notable in star-studded productions of epic scale, and in a handful of unforgettable disaster and action films.

Kennedy admits: "My favorite disaster films of all time are the *Airport* series. I receive more recognition as 'Patroni' than as anyone else, and happily so. I've enjoyed making them and they mean a lot to me."

1. AIRPORT (1970)
   Director: George Seaton; Burt Lancaster, Dean Martin, Kennedy, Helen Hayes, Jacqueline Bisset, Van Heflin.
2. AIRPORT 1975 (1974)
   D: Jack Smight; Charlton Heston, Karen Black, Kennedy, Efrem Zimbalist, Jr.
3. AIRPORT '77 (1977)
   D: Jerry Jameson; Jack Lemmon, Lee Grant, Kennedy, Brenda Vaccaro, James Stewart.
4. THE CONCORDE—AIRPORT '79 (1979)
   D: David Lowell; Alain Delon, Susan Blakely, Robert Wagner, Kennedy.
5. EARTHQUAKE (1974)
   D: Mark Robson; Charlton Heston, Ava Gardner, Kennedy, Genevieve Bujold.
   "My whole life, I always wanted to meet Ava Gardner, and I got to meet her making this picture. It was fun for me. A lot of critics shafted the living bejeezuz out of it, but it wasn't anywhere as bad as they said. A lot of people loved it. I think the special-effects guys really went crazy on it and the destruction of Los Angeles was nothing short of spectacular. The special effects in the *Airport* pictures were great, too. Sometimes the critics smell flowers that don't grow."

6. POSEIDON ADVENTURE (1972)
D: Ronald Neame; Gene Hackman, Ernest Borgnine, Red Buttons, Carol Lynley, Shelley Winters, Jack Albertson.

"It was actually pretty good. I didn't hate it; in fact, the first time I saw it, I didn't think it was that bad. It was far better than *The Towering Inferno* (1974) where they just burned that building for the sake of burning that building."

7. TRANS-ATLANTIC TUNNEL (1935)
D: Maurice Elvey; Richard Dix, Madge Evans, C. Aubrey Smith, George Arliss, Walter Huston.

"This was my favorite when I was a kid. What a picture, building this huge tunnel under the ocean. The futuristic sets were sensational. Some of those images have stayed with me all these years."

8. THE SWARM (1978)
D: Irwin Allen; Michael Caine, Katharine Ross, Henry Fonda, Richard Widmark.

"This is memorable as the worst disaster movie ever made. It was terrible! Calling it a bomb is the nicest thing you can say about it. It was a disaster as a disaster movie."

9. LOST HORIZON (1973)
D: Charles Jarrot; Peter Finch, Liv Ullmann, Kennedy, Charles Boyer, John Gielgud.

"This wasn't a disaster genre movie, as such, but it was a disaster in every other sense of the word. The music was a disaster; the reviews were a disaster; it was a disaster at the box office. And the question that's always asked is, 'Did you realize you were making a turkey?' Of course, you don't. Otherwise you wouldn't put people like Finch, Liv Ullmann, Boyer, and Gielgud into a movie and have them work their asses off every day for months to make a stinker. It just happens, and it hurts a lot, especially when the reviews are as devastating as they were for *Lost Horizon*. You know, nobody ever plays any of the music from the picture. There were ten songs by Burt Bacharach and Hal David, and they're no slouches, but they just bombed out. I'll bet you can't name a single song from the score. I was in the picture and I can't. Ross Hunter is a marvelous producer, and a personal friend, but somehow nothing worked."

GEORGE KENNEDY'S 5 FAVORITE FLICKS OF ALL TIME

Kennedy: "The fact of the matter is that *Lost Horizon* was personally disappointing to me because the original picture with Ronald Colman is one of my favorite pictures of all time."

Margo (as in Garbo) and Ronald Colman in the classic version of *Lost Horizon* (1937). The 1973 remake was an unintentional disaster film.

1. LOST HORIZON (1937)
   Director: Frank Capra; Ronald Colman, Jane Wyatt, John Howard, Edward Everett Horton, Sam Jaffe, Thomas Mitchell.
2. SINGIN' IN THE RAIN (1952)
   D: Gene Kelly, Stanley Donen; Gene Kelly, Debbie Reynolds, Donald O'Connor, Cyd Charisse.
3. CHARADE (1963)
   D: Stanley Donen; Cary Grant, Audrey Hepburn, Walter Matthau, James Coburn, Kennedy.

"I just happened to be in it, and it turned out to be one of my favorite films."

4. SHANE (1953)

D: George Stevens; Alan Ladd, Jean Arthur, Van Heflin, Brandon de Wilde.

"But you can't see this one a hundred times like you can *Charade*. It doesn't wear as well in repetition but it's still one helluva classic."

5. KING KONG (1933)

D: Merian C. Cooper; Ernest B. Schoedsack; Fay Wray, Bruce Cabot, Robert Armstrong. "The animators were about two generations ahead of their time. It's a simply super film, even today. If it was a mistake to remake *Lost Horizon,* it was a tragic error to remake *Kong* the way De Laurentiis did."

Kennedy explains: "After this the list gets a bit muddled because our tastes change as we grow from one age into another. When I was a kid my favorite pictures would've had Dick Powell and Ruby Keeler in them. When I was a little bitty boy, they might've been with Boris Karloff. When I was in my twenties, it would've been films with June Allyson and Jeanne Crain. When I was in my thirties, it changed again. But—the constants, like the foregoing five, remain. They transcend our changing tastes. That's what makes them classics.

"Today, the films I respond to are the Woody Allen pictures, Mel Brooks, Peter Sellers—Lord rest his soul—and the *Pink Panther* movies. I find they wear well with me for all of the silliness in them. At my age right now, I don't want to sit in a theatre and have more problems dealt to me than I already have in real life. And that's why I think that movies like *The Deer Hunter* (1979)—which is a marvelous film by Michael Cimino—don't do too well at the box office—because people have enough problems to deal with. They're depressed enough already. But when you come along with a piece of insanity the way Brooks does, it grabs me and the public as well. I like to laugh. I want to be entertained. And that's the best reason for going to see a movie."

GEORGE KENNEDY'S LIST OF 9 FAVORITE "HEAVIES"

1. WALTER HUSTON

"Scratch" in *The Devil and Daniel Webster,* also known as *All That Money Can Buy* (1941)

"He scared the hell out of me. (He's also my favorite actor.)"

2. MARGARET HAMILTON

The Wicked Witch of the North in *The Wizard of Oz* (1939). "She scared out what was left."

3. EDWARD ARNOLD
4. JOSEPH CALLEIA
5. PORTER HALL
6. BORIS KARLOFF
7. RICHARD WIDMARK
8. SYDNEY GREENSTREET
9. GALE SONDERGAARD

"I love 'em all, and am proud to be one of them."

JOCK MAHONEY'S LIST OF 16 ACTORS WHO HAVE DONE THEIR OWN STUNTS

Stuntman-turned-leading man Jock Mahoney is probably best known for his stint as the movie Tarzan (1962–63), and as TV's "The Range Rider" (1951–53) and "Yancy Derringer" (1958–59). He began doubling for big-name actors in the early 1940s, but was soon doing

Stuntman-turned-actor Jock Mahoney shows the way to Charles Starrett as the Durango Kid in *Laramie* (1952). Mahoney had been doubling Starrett for several years at this point.

acting parts because, as Burt Reynolds said, "Jocko was too big (6′ 4″) and too damn handsome not to get his kisser on the screen." In his countless movie and TV roles, Jock has always done his own stunts.

Says Mahoney: "Doing your own stunts adds to the realism and adds to the audience's enjoyment. For an actor, it adds a little spice to the performance. But most of all, it's a lot of fun.

"A lot of the old-time actors got their start in the business doing stuntwork and then went on to become leading men. In the twenties, two young guys named Gary Cooper and Walter Brennan climbed over the wall at the Fox Studio and got themselves hired doing saddle falls for five dollars a day. That's how they broke into films. Guys like Dave Sharpe and Dick Farnsworth were superb stuntmen, maybe the best ever, who were good looking enough to build substantial acting careers. Here are sixteen guys I've worked with who have either started out doing stuntwork or have done a fair share of their action on the screen."

1. DAVE SHARPE
2. DICK FARNSWORTH
3. BURT REYNOLDS
4. BOB FULLER
5. RON ELY
6. BEN JOHNSON
7. JIMMY GARNER
8. GEORGE O'BRIEN
9. DICK JONES
10. WALTER BRENNAN
11. GARY COOPER
12. GEORGE MONTGOMERY
13. BOB STEELE
14. CLINT EASTWOOD
15. JOHN WAYNE
16. BURT LANCASTER

CLINT EASTWOOD'S LIST OF 4 FAVORITE PERFORMANCES BY AN ACTOR

In addition to being the number-one box-office star in the world for the 1970s, Eastwood is also a film buff of the first order and can discuss the strengths and weaknesses of filmmakers around the world. Naturally, he casts a critical eye at actors' performances (including his own).

Trying to pinpoint some favorites, he says: "I'd have to say for specific performances, because I've seen product by actors I respect that wasn't very good. When I was a kid, I used to love James Cagney, but I've seen him in parts that weren't interesting to me. We've all been miscast somewhere along the line." Then with the famous Eastwood grin, he adds: "I'm able to avoid getting miscast now."

1. ALBERT FINNEY in *Saturday Night and Sunday Morning* (1960)
   "He was fantastic as this angry young man who, in a burst of noncon-
   formity, changes the lives of his girlfriends. His performance is one of my
   all-time favorites."
2. OSKAR WERNER in *The Last Ten Days of Hitler* (1956)
3. OSKAR WERNER in *Decision Before Dawn* (1951)
   "Werner's work is exceptional. I thought he was marvelous in these two
   films, much better, in fact, than the material he had to work with."
4. MONTGOMERY CLIFT in *The Search* (1948)
   "He did a beautiful job. His best work by far."

Concludes Eastwood: "These are four performances that stand
out in my mind as being something really special."

CLINT EASTWOOD'S LIST OF 7
FAVORITE ACTRESSES

Eastwood: "It's really hard to pinpoint specifics like this because there
are so many really talented ladies who I enjoy watching. A few do
stand out, but these aren't necessarily in any kind of order."

1. MAGGIE SMITH
   "I've always liked her a lot."
2. SIMONE SIGNORET
   "Her work in *Room at the Top* (1959) is unforgettable."
3. ANNA MAGNANI
   "Some of her early films like *Open City* (1945) and *The Miracle* (1950)
   are wonderful."
4. FLORINDA BALKAN
   "I enjoyed her in Vittorio De Sica's *Brief Vacation* (1975)."

   . . . And I've been lucky to work with some really fine actresses":

5. JESSICA WALTERS
   Play Misty for Me (1971)
6. VERNA BLOOM
   High Plains Drifter (1973)
7. SONDRA LOCKE
   The Outlaw Josey Wales (1976)
   The Gauntlet (1978)
   Every Which Way but Loose (1979)
   Bronco Billy (1980)
   Any Which Way You Can (1980)

Cary Grant made an unlikely WAC in *I Was a Male War Bride* (1949), which was directed by one of his favorite directors, Howard Hawks.

CARY GRANT'S 6 FAVORITE DIRECTORS

Although an Oscar for Best Actor eluded him, Cary Grant was voted a Special Academy Award in 1969 for his "unique mastery of the art of screenacting with the respect and affection of his colleagues." In his acceptance speech, he paid tribute to his favorite directors.

Said Grant: "You know, I may never look at this without remembering the quiet patience of the directors who were so kind to me, who were kind enough to put up with me more than once—some of them even three or four times."

1. ALFRED HITCHCOCK
   Suspicion (1941); *Notorious* (1946); *To Catch a Thief* (1955); *North by Northwest* (1959)
2. LEO McCAREY
   The Awful Truth (1937); *Once Upon a Honeymoon* (1942); *An Affair to Remember* (1957)
3. HOWARD HAWKS
   Bringing Up Baby (1938); *Only Angels Have Wings* (1939); *His Girl Friday* (1940); *I Was a Male War Bride* (1949); *Monkey Business* (1952)
4. GEORGE STEVENS
   Gunga Din (1939); *Penny Serenade* (1941), for which Grant received his first Oscar nomination (his second nomination came for *None but the Lonely Heart,* directed by Clifford Odets, 1944); *Talk of the Town* (1942)
5. GEORGE CUKOR
   Sylvia Scarlett (1936); *Holiday* (1938); *The Philadelphia Story* (1940)
6. STANLEY DONEN
   Kiss Them for Me (1957); *Indiscreet* (1958); *The Grass Is Greener* (1960); *Charade* (1963)

DINA MERRILL'S LIST OF 9 LADIES OF THE SILVER SCREEN WITH PANACHE

"Panache" is defined by Webster as "dash or flamboyance in style and action." Dina Merrill, leading lady and socialite, is another definition of panache. She has been lending class to dozens of films since the 1950s, notably, *The Desk Set* (1957), *The Sundowners* (1959), *The Courtship of Eddie's Father* (1963), *I'll Take Sweden* (1965), *The Greatest* (1977), and *A Wedding* (1978).

Says Merrill: "Here are eight ladies with a lot of panache, whose class and style are timeless."

1. KATHARINE HEPBURN
2. MYRNA LOY
3. CLAUDETTE COLBERT
4. VERA MILES
5. GENA ROWLANDS
6. ELLEN BURSTYN
7. JANE ALEXANDER
8. MERYL STREEP
9. BLYTHE DANNER

9 CABARET

CHAPTER

Or: *There's Music and Laughter in the Air*

BUDDY EBSEN'S LIST OF THE DANCINGEST FEET IN THE SINGIN' AND DANCIN' MOVIES OF HOLLYWOOD'S GOLDEN AGE

To TV fans it is not common knowledge that Buddy Ebsen began his professional career in vaudeville days as a dancer, teaming with his sister Vilma in 1928. Says Ebsen: "For several years, Vilma and I were the poor man's Fred Astaire and Ginger Rogers on the nightclub circuit, road tours, and in a string of stage musicals, culminating in *Flying Colors,* one of the top revues of 1932."

Hollywood beckoned, and Buddy signed with MGM to dance and sing his way through such "all-talking, all-singing, all-dancing" musicals as *Broadway Melody of 1936, Captain January* (1936), *Banjo on My Knee* (l936), *Girl of the Golden West* (1937), and *Broadway Melody of 1938.*

Ebsen allows: "I was making $2,000 a week in 1938, but it was like bondage. One day Louis B. Mayer called me into his office and said, 'Ebsen, in order for us to give you the kind of parts you deserve, we must own you.' I thought about it for a minute, but I didn't like the sound of the word *own.* So I answered, 'I'll tell you what kind of fool I am, Mr. Mayer, I can't be owned.' And I walked out of his office, wondering if I really was a fool."

In the Movieland of 1938, you didn't say no to the king cheese when he offered you a great big glamorous bubble for your puny little soul. Ebsen then left Hollywood, and returned only occasionally for pictures over the next sixteen years. "In spite of a few rough years, I never regretted my decision."

1. FRED ASTAIRE
   "He had no equal."
2. GEORGE MURPHY
   "Senator George Murphy was a good hoofer."
3. BILL "BOJANGLES" ROBINSON
   "When we used to play benefits in New York, I'd go to the Palace to watch him, and steal all the steps that I could. He was somebody I tried to emulate. Course, we had completely different styles. He was a tap dancer, and my style and body movement was . . . a little eccentric." (Walt Disney said that Ebsen always reminded him of a life-size dancing puppet.)
4. JIMMY CAGNEY
   "He was surprisingly good, but then he had a dancing background. He started out, like I did, in a chorus line in a Broadway show. Actually it was Forty-second Street, but it was known as Broadway. My first show was *Whoopee* in 1928, a Ziegfeld production with Eddie Cantor."

Buddy Ebsen and Shirley Temple square off for a dancing duet in *Captain January* (1936).

5. ELEANOR POWELL
   "We danced together in *Broadway Melody of 1936* and *Born to Dance* (1936). She sure had vitality, and legs to knock your eyes out."
6. ANN MILLER
   "She was marvelous, and still is. Dancing as good as ever in *Sugar Babies* on Broadway now, with Mickey Rooney. It's the biggest hit in New York."
7. SHIRLEY TEMPLE
   "You know, for her age, she was a great little hoofer. She could pick up steps like it was nothing. She was a quick study and could execute some really difficult steps. We did *Captain January* together."
8. JOHN BUBBLES (of the act known as Buck and Bubbles)
   "I don't know if he ever made any pictures, but if he didn't, he should have. He was a superb dancer, very popular in New York. He was someone else I tried to emulate."
9. GENE KELLY
   "Course he came later than most of these others, but he was one of the best."

DICK MARTIN'S 10 FAVORITE MOVIE COMEDIES

Says Martin: "Not necessarily in this order. You'll notice that I didn't include my biggie, *The Maltese Bippy* (1966). Thought I'd leave that one for somebody else's list."

1. THE PHILADELPHIA STORY (1940)
   Director: George Cukor; Cary Grant, Katharine Hepburn, James Stewart (who won Best Actor Academy Award)
2. TO BE OR NOT TO BE (1942)
   D: Ernest Lubitsch; Jack Benny, Carole Lombard, Robert Stack, Sig Ruman
3. NOTHING SACRED (1937)
   D: William Welman; Carole Lombard, Fredric March, Walter Connolly, Sig Ruman
4. DR. STRANGELOVE, OR: HOW I LEARNED TO STOP WORRYING AND LOVE THE BOMB (1964)
   D: Stanley Kubrick; Peter Sellers, George C. Scott, Sterling Hayden, Slim Pickens, Keenan Wynn
5. LA CAGE AUX FOLLES (BIRDS OF A FEATHER) (1979)
   D: Edouard Molinaro; Ugo Tognazzi, Michel Serrault. Oscar winner for Best Foreign Film.
6. ANNIE HALL (1977)
   D: Woody Allen; Woody Allen, Diane Keaton, Tony Roberts, Paul Simon. Oscar winner for Best Picture, Best Actress, Best Director, Best Screenplay (Allen and Marshall Brickman).

James Stewart, Cary Grant, and Katharine Hepburn, in the 1940 comedy classic, *The Philadelphia Story,* for which Stewart won an Oscar.

7. WHERE'S POPPA? (1970)
   D: Carl Reiner; George Segal, Ruth Gordon, Trish Van Devere, Ron Leibman
8. UNFAITHFULLY YOURS (1948)
   D: Preston Sturges; Rex Harrison, Linda Darnell, Barbara Lawrence, Rudy Vallee. "Peter Sellers told me before his death that he wanted to remake this picture. It could have been great."
9. THE BANK DICK (1940)
   D: Eddie Cline; W. C. Fields, Cora Witherspoon, Una Merkel, Evelyn Del Rio
10. NIGHT AT THE OPERA (1935)
   D: Sam Wood; Groucho, Chico, and Harpo Marx, Kitty Carlisle, Allan Jones, Sig Ruman

FRED MacMURRAY'S LIST OF 10 CLASSIC DISNEY FAMILY COMEDIES

For many years, Fred MacMurray, who debuted in films in 1934 with *Friends of Mr. Sweeney,* was one of Hollywood's highest paid actors. He had no formal training except as a saxophonist, yet turned in memorable performances in such films as *Trail of the Lonesome Pine* (1936), *Double Indemnity* (1944), *The Egg and I* (1947), and *The Caine Mutiny* (1954). He switched successfully from light comedy to action to melodrama, and in later years found a new home at the Walt Disney Studios as the star of a handful of top-grossing family comedies.

Admits MacMurray: "They were just plain fun. Fun to do and fun to watch. Nobody could make a family picture like Walt could. The films Walt made are still as great today. Some are real classics, and the fact that I was in a bunch of them didn't hurt them all that much. They're fun to watch anyway."

1. THE SHAGGY DOG (1959)
   MacMurray, Jean Hagen, Annette Funicello. "This was Walt's first slapstick comedy. It was about a boy, Tommy Kirk, who turns into a sheepdog through an ancient spell."
2. THE ABSENT-MINDED PROFESSOR (1961)
   MacMurray, Nancy Olson, Ed Wynn. "This is the picture where I discover flubber—that's flying rubber. We did some great gags with it."
3. PARENT TRAP(1961)
   Brian Keith, Maureen O'Hara, Hayley Mills. "Hayley played two parts—twins who were trying to get their divorced parents back together."
4. SON OF FLUBBER (1963)
   MacMurray, Nancy Olson, Keenan Wynn, Tommy Kirk. "This was the

Fred MacMurray was at his zany best in Walt Disney's *Son of Flubber* (1963), with Nancy Olson.

sequel to *Absent-Minded Professor*. I had some crazy new inventions—flubbergas and dry rain.''

5. THAT DARN CAT (1965)
   Hayley Mills, Dean Jones, Dorothy Provine
6. FOLLOW ME, BOYS! (1966)
   MacMurray, Vera Miles, Kurt Russell
7. THE UGLY DACHSHUND (1966)
   Dean Jones, Suzanne Pleshette, Charlie Ruggles
8. BLACKBEARD'S GHOST (1967)
   Peter Ustinov, Dean Jones, Suzanne Pleshette

9. MONKEYS GO HOME (1967)
   Maurice Chevalier, Dean Jones, Yvette Mimieux
10. THE LOVE BUG (1969)
    Dean Jones, Michele Lee, Buddy Hackett

DEBBIE REYNOLDS' LIST OF 11 UNFORGETTABLE MUSICAL NUMBERS

Vivacious and effervescent, Debbie Reynolds, whose film debut was in *The Daughter of Rosie O'Grady* (1950), won early fame as a young leading lady in the musicals of the 1950s. She has the distinction of having starred in *Singin' in the Rain* (1952), which has been chosen by critics to be the finest musical ever made. Following her string of musicals, she went on to develop into a fine screen comedienne, returning occasionally to the movie musical for such successes as *The Unsinkable Molly Brown* (1964) and *The Singing Nun* (1966). In recent years, she has successfully made the transition to becoming a Las Vegas headliner, with an act in which she creates musical numbers which recall some of her magical moments on the silver screen.

1. ANN MILLER in *Small Town Girl* (1953)
   "She does an eye-popping 'I've Gotta Hear That Beat' number staged by Busby Berkeley, where hands erupt from the dance floor to play musical instruments. It's a classic."
2. ELEANOR POWELL and FRED ASTAIRE in *Broadway Melody of 1940*
   "Their breathtaking tap routine on the highly polished black marble floor."
3. LESLIE CARON and GENE KELLY in *An American in Paris* (1951)
   "The whole thing, but especially the boulevard number."
4. DONALD O'CONNOR in the "Make 'Em Laugh" number in *Singin' in the Rain* (1952)
5. JUDY GARLAND "dancing down the yellow brick road with the Tin Man (Jack Haley), the Scarecrow (Ray Bolger), and the cowardly Lion (Bert Lahr) in *The Wizard of Oz* (1939)."
6. RITA HAYWORTH
   "She was never sexier than when singing "Put the Blame on Mame" in *Gilda* (1946)."
7. CYD CHARISSE and FRED ASTAIRE in the twelve-minute highlight of *The Band Wagon* (1953)
   A private-eye ballet called "The Girl Hunt."
8. BILL "BOJANGLES" ROBINSON dancing with SHIRLEY TEMPLE in *The Little Colonel* (1935)
   The famous staircase routine.

9. FRED ASTAIRE and GINGER ROGERS at their best in *Top Hat* (1935) In "Cheek to Cheek," "Isn't This a Lovely Day To Be Caught in the Rain?" and "Top Hat, White Tie, and Tails."
10. JUDY GARLAND singing "Have Yourself a Merry Little Christmas" to Margaret O'Brien in *Meet Me in St. Louis* (1944).
11. ELEANOR POWELL's sensational footwork to "I've Got You Under My Skin" in *Born to Dance* (1936) "And most of her other great musical numbers at MGM."

DEBBIE REYNOLDS' LIST OF THE 8 BEST MALE DANCERS IN THE MOVIES

1. GENE KELLY
2. FRED ASTAIRE
3. DONALD O'CONNOR
4. GENE NELSON
5. GOWER CHAMPION
6. BILL "BOJANGLES" ROBINSON
7. and 8. THE NICHOLAS BROTHERS
"Two black dancers who are without a doubt the greatest acrobatic dancers ever. Catch them in *The Pirate* (1948)."

DEBBIE REYNOLDS' LIST OF THE 9 BEST FEMALE DANCERS IN THE MOVIES

1. ELEANOR POWELL
2. ANN MILLER
3. JULIET PROWSE
4. MARGE CHAMPION
5. CYD CHARISSE
6. GWEN VERDON
7. VERA-ELLEN
8. LESLIE CARON
9. RITA HAYWORTH

DEBBIE REYNOLDS' LIST OF HER 8 FAVORITE MUSICALS

1. MEET ME IN ST. LOUIS (1944)
Director: Vincente Minnelli; Judy Garland, Margaret O'Brien, Mary Astor, Lucille Bremer, Marjorie Main, June Lockhart, Harry Davenport, Tom Drake. "A wonderful picture."
2. GIGI (1958)
D: Vincente Minnelli; Leslie Caron, Maurice Chevalier, Louis Jourdan, Eva Gabor. Winner of nine Academy Awards, including Best Picture, Best Director, Best Writing, Best Song, and Best Musical Score. "A must see!"

minutive superstar Shirley Temple and Bill "Bojangles" Robinson do his nous stair dance in *The Little Colonel* (1935).

Debbie Reynolds and Harve Presnell in a rousing musical number from *The Unsinkable Molly Brown* (1964).

3. SINGIN' IN THE RAIN (1952)
   D: Gene Kelly, Stanley Donen; Kelly, Donald O'Connor, Reynolds, Jean Hagen, Cyd Charisse. "Although it won no Oscars, it's one of the best ever made."
4. HELLO, DOLLY (1969)
   D: Gene Kelly; Barbra Streisand, Walter Matthau, Michael Crawford, E. J. Peaker, Louis Armstrong. Winner of three Academy Awards, including Best Musical Score.
5. THE UNSINKABLE MOLLY BROWN (1964)
   D: Charles Walters; Reynolds, Harve Presnell, Ed Begley, Jack Kruschen, Hermione Baddeley. Won five Oscar nominations. "Can't help it, it's one of my favorites."
6. FUNNY GIRL (1968)
   D: William Wyler; Barbra Streisand, Omar Sharif, Kay Medford, Anne

Francis, Walter Pidgeon. Streisand's Academy Award-winning motion picture debut. She shared the Oscar win with Katharine Hepburn for *The Lion in Winter,* with whom she tied.

7. TIN PAN ALLEY (1940)
   D: Walter Lang; Alice Faye, Betty Grable, Jack Oakie, John Payne, Billy Gilbert, Allen Jenkins, Nicholas Brothers. "Not so much for itself, but more for the fact that this picture was representative of all the great Alice Faye and Betty Grable musicals of the forties. They were *the* blondes in movie musicals, and they were the greatest!"

8. TOP HAT (1935)
   D: Mark Sandrich; Fred Astaire, Ginger Rogers, Edward Everett Horton. "Although this is a knockout musical and probably the best of Astaire and Rogers, it's also the best example of the thirties musicals, right through the typical mistaken identity plot. It represents all of the musicals I love from the thirties, as *Tin Pan Alley* does for the forties."

DAVID ROSE'S LIST OF 9 MEMORABLE MOVIE MUSICAL SCORES

Although his greatest fame has come as composer/conductor on "The Red Skelton Show" for twenty-seven years (on both radio and TV), David Rose is also a potent name in motion picture scoring. He began composing for films in 1941, and won two Academy Award nominations: one for scoring *The Prince and the Pirate* (1944), and then for the song "So In Love" for *Wonder Man* (1945). In the 1950s, while under contract to MGM for eight years, he scored dozens of films like *The Girl Who Had Everything* (1953), with Elizabeth Taylor, and *The Clown* (1953), with Red Skelton.

Maintains Rose: "If you go back to the old days, you've got the cream of the crop. Almost anything that Max Steiner or Victor Young did was great. And there's no end to those; between them they must've scored 600 movies, maybe more."

1. GONE WITH THE WIND (1939)
   Clark Gable, Vivien Leigh; music, Max Steiner. "It was nominated for Best Original Score, and really should've won, but he lost to *The Wizard of Oz.*"

2. SINCE YOU WENT AWAY (1944)
   Claudette Colbert, Jennifer Jones, Joseph Cotten; music, Max Steiner. "He won the Oscar this time for Best Scoring of a Dramatic or Comedy Picture."

3. SPELLBOUND (1945)

Ingrid Bergman, Gregory Peck; music, Miklos Rosza. Won the Academy Award for Best Scoring of a Dramatic or Comedy Picture.

4. AROUND THE WORLD IN 80 DAYS (1956)
David Niven, Shirley MacLaine, Cantinflas; music, Victor Young. Won the Academy Award for Best Score of a Dramatic or Comedy Picture.

5. LAWRENCE OF ARABIA (1962)
Peter O'Toole, Omar Sharif, Alec Guinness; music, Maurice Jarre. Won the Academy Award for Best Original Score.

6. DR. ZHIVAGO (1965)
Omar Sharif, Julie Christie; music, Maurice Jarre. Won the Academy Award for Best Original Score.

7. THE THOMAS CROWN AFFAIR (1968)
Steve McQueen, Faye Dunaway; music, Michel Legrand; song, "The Windmills of Your Mind," by Legrand, lyrics by Marilyn and Alan Bergman; sung by Noel Harrison. Won the Academy Award for Best Song.

8. BRIAN'S SONG (1970)
Billy Dee Williams, James Cann. "This TV movie was so successful that it was released to theatres in 1971, and did fair business. Its beautiful score is by Michel Legrand."

9. THE WAY WE WERE (1973)
Robert Redford, Barbra Streisand; music, Marvin Hamlisch; title song by Hamlisch, lyrics by Alan and Marilyn Bergman; sung by Barbra Streisand. Won Oscars for both Best Song and Best Original Dramatic Score.

SHIRLEY JONES' LIST OF THE 10 BEST MOVIE ADAPTATIONS OF BROADWAY MUSICALS

Though best known in recent years for her successful TV comedy series, "The Partridge Family" (1970–74), Shirley Jones is an Oscar-winning film star. Her performance in *Elmer Gantry* (1960) won her an Academy Award as Best Supporting Actress, which was quite a feat since her career sprung from Broadway musical comedy. Her film debut was as the female lead in *Oklahoma!* (1955), which was followed by *Carousel* (1956). In addition to these two nearly flawless movie adaptations of Broadway hits, she also costarred with Robert Preston in *The Music Man* (1962).

Says Jones: "Here's my list . . . in reverse order."

10. THE UNSINKABLE MOLLY BROWN (1964)
Director: Charles Walters; Debbie Reynolds, Harve Presnell, Ed Begley, Jack Kruschen, Hermione Baddeley

9. AUNTIE MAME (1958)
D: Morton DaCosta; Rosalind Russell, Forrest Tucker, Coral Browne, Fred Clark, Roger Smith, Patric Knowles, Joanna Barnes

8. CAMELOT (1967)
   D: Joshua Logan; Richard Harris, Vanessa Redgrave, Franco Nero, David Hemmings, Lionel Jeffries
7. GREASE (1978)
   D: Randal Kleiser; John Travolta, Olivia Newton-John, Stockard Channing, Jeff Conaway, Didi Conn, Eve Arden, Sid Caesar
6. MY FAIR LADY (1964)
   D: George Cukor; Rex Harrison, Audrey Hepburn, Stanley Holloway, Wilfrid Hyde-White, Gladys Cooper, Theodore Bikel
5. HELLO, DOLLY! (1969)
   D: Gene Kelly; Barbra Streisand, Walter Matthau, Michael Crawford, E. J. Peaker, Louis Armstrong
4. CAROUSEL (1956)
   D: Henry King; Gordon MacRae, Shirley Jones, Cameron Mitchell, Barbara Ruick, Gene Lockhart
3. GYPSY (1962)
   D: Mervyn LeRoy; Rosalind Russell, Natalie Wood, Karl Malden, Paul Wallace, Betty Bruce, Parley Baer, Harry Shannon
2. THE MUSIC MAN (1962)
   D: Morton DaCosta; Robert Preston, Shirley Jones, Buddy Hackett, Hermione Gingold, Paul Ford
1. OKLAHOMA! (1955)
   D: Fred Zinneman; Gordon MacRae, Shirley Jones, Charlotte Greenwood, Rod Steiger, Gloria Grahame, Eddie Albert, James Whitmore, Gene Nelson

Explains Jones: "I don't mean to seem self-serving by putting three of my films on this list, but I truly feel that these movie adaptations, disregarding my part in them, are among the best that have been done."

JOHN RITTER'S LIST OF 18 OF THE MOST OUTRAGEOUS COMEDIES OF RECENT VINTAGE

TV superstar John Ritter, of ABC's "Three's Company" (1977–present), appreciates outrageous comedy. Says he: "Subtle comedy is okay, but you're not going to get any belly laughs unless you're outrageous. And at the same time, you can't be juvenile or play down to your audience. The setup is really important. The key is to establish a preposterous situation, and then play it straight."

1. WHERE'S POPPA? (1970)
   Director: Carl Reiner; George Segal, Ruth Gordon, Trish Van Devere, Ron Liebman

2. THE PRODUCERS (1968)
   D: Mel Brooks; Zero Mostel, Gene Wilder, Dick Shawn
3. AIRPLANE (1980)
   D: Aorahams/Zucker/Zucker; Robert Hays, Robert Stack, Lloyd Bridges
4. THE GREAT RACE (1965)
   D: Blake Edwards; Tony Curtis, Jack Lemmon, Natalie Wood, Peter Faulk
5. THE RUSSIANS ARE COMING, THE RUSSIANS ARE COMING (1966)
   D: Norman Jewison; Carl Reiner, Eva Marie Saint, Alan Arkin, Brian Keith
6. HAROLD AND MAUDE (1972)
   D: Hal Ashby; Bud Cort, Ruth Gordon, Vivian Pickles
7. IT'S A MAD, MAD, MAD, MAD WORLD (1963)
   D: Stanley Kramer; Spencer Tracy, Milton Berle, Sid Caesar
8. START THE REVOLUTION WITHOUT ME (1970)
   D: Bud Yorkin; Gene Wilder, Donald Sutherland, Hugh Griffith
9. M*A*S*H (1970)
   D: Robert Altman; Donald Sutherland, Elliott Gould, Sally Kellerman
10. EVERY WHICH WAY BUT LOOSE (1979)
    D: James Fargo; Clint Eastwood, Ruth Gordon, Sondra Locke
11. BANANAS (1971)
    D: Woody Allen; Woody Allen, Louise Lasser
12. TAKE THE MONEY AND RUN (1969)
    D: Woody Allen; Woody Allen, Janet Margolin
13. PLAY IT AGAIN, SAM (1972)
    D: Herbert Ross; Woody Allen, Diane Keaton, Tony Roberts
14. WHAT'S UP, DOC? (1972)
    D: Peter Bogdanovich; Barbra Streisand, Ryan O'Neal, Madeline Kahn
15. THE LONGEST YARD (1974)
    D: Robert Aldrich; Burt Reynolds, Eddie Albert, Ed Lauter
16. HEAVEN CAN WAIT
    D: Warren Beatty, Buck Henry; Warren Beatty, Julie Christie, Jack Warden, Dyan Cannon
17. OH, GOD! (1977)
    D: Carl Reiner; George Burns, John Denver
18. ALL of the PINK PANTHER movies
    D: Blake Edwards; Peter Sellers

10
CHAPTER

THE THRILL OF IT ALL

Or: *A Sampling of Sci-Fi, Satan, Whodunits .... and How They Did It*

FRED MacMURRAY'S LIST OF 10 CLASSIC FILMS NOIR

Film noir is a term coined by French critics for a genre of American films of the later 1930s and 1940s that deal expressly with the darker side of human nature. Literally translated, *film noir* means "black film," and the principal characters typically lack redeeming qualities. They are unsympathetic and sometimes downright unsavory; yet somehow the audience is moved into caring what happens to them. More often than not, the principals are caught up in forces which they cannot control; and more often than not, they end up losers rather than winners. The fatalism which abounds in this genre is conveyed with a heavy use of night scenes and dark shadows.

One of the great classics of this genre is *Double Indemnity* (1944), directed by Billy Wilder, written by Raymond Chandler and James Cain, and starring Barbara Stanwyck and MacMurray. The film deals with a woman who seduces an insurance salesman into a plot to murder her husband for the insurance money. Once involved, he cannot get out. And it leads to his inevitable demise.

Explains MacMurray: "Of course, in the old days, the perpetrator of any crime had to pay because of the Hays Office. They couldn't, like they do nowadays, steal the money and go to Mexico. You had to pay for any misdoing. I think the influence on our kids by pictures like that was better than it is today.''

Director Wilder says: ''Fred didn't really want to do *Indemnity*. He was afraid of what it would do to his image. Eleven other actors turned it down, and yet it brought Fred the best notices of his career. He was talked about as being a real actor.''

1. DOUBLE INDEMNITY (1944)
   Director: Billy Wilder; MacMurray, Stanwyck, Edward G. Robinson

The conniving Barbara Stanwyck tries to talk insurance salesman Fred MacMurray into committing murder in the classic *film noir, Double Indemnity* (1944).

2. OUT OF THE PAST (1947)
   D: Jacques Tourneur; Robert Mitchum, Kirk Douglas, Jane Greer, Rhonda Fleming
3. TREASURE OF THE SIERRA MADRE (1948)
   D: John Huston; Humphrey Bogart, Walter Huston, Tim Holt, Bruce Bennett. Won Oscars for Best Director and Best Supporting Actor (Walter Huston).
4. WOMAN IN THE WINDOW (1944)
   D: Fritz Lang; Joan Bennett, Edward G. Robinson, Dan Duryea, Raymond Massey, Bobby Blake
5. THE KILLERS (1946)
   D: Robert Siodmak; Burt Lancaster, Ava Gardner, Edmond O'Brien
6. HIGH SIERRA (1941)
   D: Raoul Walsh; Humphrey Bogart, Ida Lupino, Arthur Kennedy
7. D.O.A. (1949)
   D: Rudolph Mate; Edmond O'Brien, Pamela Britton, Luther Adler, Neville Brand
8. LOST WEEKEND (1945)
   D: Billy Wilder; Ray Milland, Jane Wyman, Philip Terry. Won Milland an Oscar as Best Actor.
9. THE POSTMAN ALWAYS RINGS TWICE (1946)
   D: Tay Garnett; Lana Turner, John Garfield, Cecil Kellaway, Audrey Totter
10. THE SET-UP (1949)
    D: Robert Wise; Robert Ryan, Audrey Totter, George Tobias, Wallace Ford

VERA MILES' 5 FAVORITE ALFRED HITCHCOCK FILMS

Former Miss Kansas and second runner-up in the Miss America Pageant of 1948, Vera Miles was discovered by Howard Hughes and brought to Hollywood under contract. Following years of modeling work, live TV dramas, and several minor films (like *Charge at Feather River* in 1953), she was rediscovered by Alfred Hitchcock, who put her under personal contract (1955–62). During those seven years, she made two motion pictures for him, *The Wrong Man* (1957) and *Psycho* (1960), and also starred in the television pilot for the "Alfred Hitchcock Presents" series (1955–65), as well as in several episodes of the suspense program which made Hitchcock the most famous director in the world. Also, while under contract to him, Hitchcock loaned her out for other films, notably *23 Paces to Baker Street* (1956), *The Searchers* (1956), *The FBI Story* (1959), and *The Man Who Shot Liberty Valance* (1962).

Vera Miles in her best screen scream from Alfred Hitchcock's *Psycho* (1960).

Says Miles: "Hitch was not always a pleasant man, and he liked to control people too much. I admired him as a director but we often butted heads over what was or was not right for me. He had a wry sense of humor and, as you might suspect, liked to shock and titillate people. Being British, he always had tea on his sets at 4:00, which is high tea. And while we were making *Psycho,* he insisted on having Mrs. Bates, the mummified thing that was supposed to be Tony Perkins' mother in the film, at the tea table with us. When guests were on the set, he always introduced them to Mrs. Bates, and then to Tony, who he introduced as Master Bates."

1. NOTORIOUS (1946)
   Cary Grant, Ingrid Bergman. "This is Hitch at his all-around best. He got the idea from reading a small article about some strange new element called uranium, and created a classic film about something that no one knew too much about at the time."

2. SUSPICION (1941)
   Cary Grant, Joan Fontaine. "This is probably his best use of an objective camera."
3. LIFEBOAT (1944)
   Tallulah Bankhead, William Bendix, John Hodiak. "It was an ingenious use of what was principally a single set."
4. I CONFESS (1953)
   Montgomery Clift, Karl Malden, Anne Baxter
5. DIAL M FOR MURDER (1954)
   Ray Milland, Grace Kelly, Robert Cummings

MELVIN BELLI'S LIST OF 5 FAMOUS TRIALS THAT HAVE BEEN IMMORTALIZED ON FILM

Melvin Belli is one of the most celebrated lawyers of our times. During his well-chronicled nearly fifty years of law practice, he has won hundreds of cases with award settlements exceeding $100,000 each. He has been counsel in cases tried in England, Japan, Italy, and Scandinavia, and has represented such illustrious clients as Marie McDonald, Mae West, Anne Jeffreys, Errol Flynn, Rossano Brazzi, and Tony Curtis. He is also widely remembered for his defense of Jack Ruby, on trial in Dallas for the slaying of Lee Harvey Oswald. In constant demand as a speaker and for television and radio shows, Belli travels extensively and is currently preparing to launch a TV series based on his trial cases.

Says Belli: "I have long asked why it is that we do not see more films being made about those trials over which the entire nation has kept a close and cautious watch. Perhaps the most notable fact in making the following list was the lack of socially and historically significant cases that have paved the future of our great nation."

1. INHERIT THE WIND (1960)
   "Based on the 1925 Scopes 'monkey' trial, this Stanley Kramer-directed film is unquestionably the best transformation of a real trial to the silver screen. Spencer Tracy gives an exemplary performance as the legendary defense counsel, Clarence Darrow. Fredric March gives an equally superb showing as prosecutor William Jennings Bryan. One of the most famous and significant trials of all times, the Scopes case involved a schoolteacher who was being prosecuted for teaching Darwin's theory of evolution."
2. ANATOMY OF A MURDER (1959)
   "Daring when it was first released, this gripping courtroom drama is one of Otto Preminger's best directorial efforts. It was based on a 1952 case

in which Lieutenant Peterson, an army officer, was charged with murdering a bartender after the latter assaulted the officer's wife. He was acquitted on reason of temporary insanity. James Stewart gives a commanding performance as Peterson's attorney, who in real life wrote the book from which the movie was taken, while serving as a judge on the Supreme Court of the state of Michigan. Also noteworthy is the fact that the actor, Joseph N. Welch, who played the judge, had in reality served as a judge, including a stint supervising the infamous McCarthy hearings in the fifties."

3. COMPULSION (1959)

"Directed by Richard Fleischer, this film with Orson Welles is an excellent recreation of the notorious Leopold-Loeb trial. The case involved two Chicago students who, for no other apparent reason than sport, kidnapped and murdered a young boy. Dean Stockwell and Bradford Dillman are at their best in this film."

4. CELL 2455, DEATH ROW (1955)

"This address was the long-time ·residence of alleged murderer Caryl Chessman, who staved off his execution for ten years after conviction through a series of appeals. Chessman became one of the greatest 'writ' lawyers ever during his stay in prison. William Campbell starred as Chessman, and Kathryn Grant portrayed his attorney."

5. I WANT TO LIVE (1958)

"Under Robert Wise's expert direction, Susan Hayward won an Oscar for her gutsy performance as Barbara Graham, the real-life prostitute whose life came to an end in the gas chamber amid increasing controversy and doubt as to her guilt in the murder for which she was convicted."

ERNEST BORGNINE'S LIST OF 10 MOVIE VILLAINS YOU LOVE TO HATE

Without question, Ernest Borgnine, from the moment he essayed the role of Fatso Judson in *From Here to Eternity* (1953), became a memorable movie villain you loved to hate.

States Borgnine: "These are the kind of actors I've patterned myself after in certain performances. They all have a strong physical presence and are riveting on the screen no matter what kind of role they play. When you're doing a villain, you have to pull out all the stops to make it believable. I remember when I was doing *The Revengers* (1972), with Bill Holden, I didn't have quite as firm a grip on my character as I wanted, which can ruin your performance. We were down in Mexico, and I got a call from home and found out that my ex-wife was suing me for divorce. It was a blessing in disguise, in that the way I coped with the anxiety of the situation was that I patterned my character after *her*. I ended up playing her on the screen, and it's one of my meanest, dirtiest roles *ever*."

1. STROTHER MARTIN
2. LEE MARVIN
3. JACK PALANCE
4. RICHARD WIDMARK
5. JACK ELAM
6. BASIL RATHBONE
7. CLAUDE RAINS
8. HUMPHREY BOGART
9. EDDIE G. ROBINSON
10. JIMMY CAGNEY

FORREST J. ACKERMAN'S LIST OF THE 11 KINGS OF HORROR FILMS

The least of Forrest J. Ackerman's achievements over the years is his coining of the phrase "sci-fi" in 1954, which, much to his delight, has become universally popular. He has seized for himself the mantle of the World's Greatest Science Fiction Fan (and that includes horror, fantasy, and occult).

His love affair with science fiction began in 1926 at age nine, and he has since collected enough memorabilia, artifacts, and books to fill his entire four-story, seventeen-room house—called "The Ackermansion"—literally to the rafters. His entire collection, worth millions, was donated to the City of Los Angeles, which will build a museum to house and properly display it.

Forry is best known to his fans as the editor of the *Famous Monsters of Filmland* magazine, which he originated in 1958 and which is still going strong. He takes pride in having published Ray Bradbury's first story (in *Imagination* in 1938). Not a man to limit his activities, Forry is a literary agent, an author, book editor, translator, lecturer, anthologist, senior editor of the *Perry Rhodan* paperback series, the director of the Science Fiction Agency, the founder of the Fantasy Foundation and the Ackerman Archives, and the very first winner of the science fiction literary award, The Hugo, in 1952. He has also won dozens of other awards.

And, of course, Forrest J. Ackerman knows his horror movies. He says the following stars were the greatest! . . . in alphabetical order.

1. JOHN CARRADINE
2. LON CHANEY, JR.
3. LON CHANEY, SR.
4. PETER CUSHING
5. BORIS KARLOFF
6. CHRISTOPHER LEE
7. PETER LORRE
8. BELA LUGOSI
9. CLAUDE RAINS
10. CONRAD VEIDT
11. PAUL WEGENER

Boris Karloff, who became immortalized as Frankenstein's monster after the part was turned down by both Bela Lugosi and John Carradine, went on to become one of the kings of the horror film.

... AND 3 QUEENS OF THE SILVER SCREAM

1. ELSA LANCHESTER
2. BARBARA STEELE
3. FAY WRAY

STEPHEN KING'S LIST OF THE 6 SCARIEST SCENES EVER CAPTURED ON FILM

The author of such best-selling novels of terror as *Carrie, Salem's Lot, Night Shift, The Stand, The Shining, The Dead Zone,* and *Fire Starter,* Stephen King is the undisputed modern master of the macabre. His imagery is highly visual, revealing an early and strong influence by movies. Although he has probably instilled more fear in the hearts of readers than any other contemporary writer, he, too, has experienced chilling moments in the darkness of a theatre.

1. WAIT UNTIL DARK (1967)
    Director: Terence Young; Audrey Hepburn, Alan Arkin, Richard Crenna. "The moment near the conclusion, when Arkin jumps out at Audrey Hepburn, is a real scare."
2. CARRIE (1976)
    D: Brian de Palma; Sissy Spacek, Piper Laurie, William Katt, John Travolta, Amy Irving. "The dream sequence at the end, when Sissy Spacek thrusts her hand out of the ground and grabs Amy Irving. I knew it was coming and I still felt as if I'd swallowed a snowcone whole."
3. I BURY THE LIVING (1958)
    D: Albert Band; Richard Boone, Theodore Bikel. "In this almost-forgotten movie, there is a chilling sequence when Boone begins to maniacally remove the black pins in the filled graveyard plots and to replace them with white pins."
4. THE TEXAS CHAINSAW MASSACRE (1974)
    D: Tobe Hooper; Marilyn Burns, Allen Danziger. "The moment when the corpse seems to leap out of the freezer like a hideous jack-in-the-box."
5. NIGHT OF THE LIVING DEAD (1968)
    D: George Romero; Judith O'Dea, Russell Streiner. "The scene where the little girl stabs her mother to death with a garden trowel in the cellar . . . 'Mother, please, I can do it myself.' "
6. PSYCHO (1960)
    D: Alfred Hitchcock; Tony Perkins, Janet Leigh, Vera Miles. "The shower scene, of course."

ANTON LA VEY'S LIST OF 10 HIGHLY SATANIC SCREEN PORTRAYALS

A man with many talents and a richly varied background of experience, Anton La Vey is best known as the High Priest of the international Church of Satan, which he founded in 1966. The purpose of the Church, he says, "combines a study and exposition of historical legends and traditions about Satan with a very temporal philosophy of attaining physical and financial success in the present."

In his half-century, La Vey has worked as a police photographer, an architectural draftsman, an oboist with the San Francisco Ballet Orchestra, an animal trainer with Clyde Beatty, a film actor and consultant; and in his late teens and early twenties he was an accomplished organist playing at burlesque houses, movie theatres, taverns, and convention halls. He's well-read and well-versed on such unrelated topics as the history of the dirigible, the fine points of a magician's act, the ironies of the legend of Marilyn Monroe (with whom he had a brief affair in 1948), and, of course, the movies. He's a lifelong cinema buff.

States La Vey: "Actors who usually attempt satanic portrayals deliver these histrionic performances, and are often pretentious and come off meaningless. The ones I've chosen for my list are characterizations which are proud, defiant, sympathetic, and sometimes tragic. Their lines and speeches are meaningful. At best, you could say that many of them are typical anti-heroic *film noir* characters."

1. EDWARD G. ROBINSON in *The Sea Wolf* (1941)
   "Probably one of the most satanic portrayals ever done on the screen, in Miltonian terms. Throughout *Sea Wolf* there are allusions to *Paradise Lost*. In Wolf Larsen's library, Milton's book is open to the passage: 'Better to reign in hell than to serve in heaven,' which not only sets up this picture, but is a key to most of the others on this list. Wolf Larsen, if you'll remember, only degrades those who have already degraded themselves; he brutalizes only those who know only brutalization; he preys upon those who deserve to be preyed upon. Robinson, in this, is a purely satanic figure."

2. EDWARD G. ROBINSON in *Key Largo* (1948)
   "Here, Robinson's a very self-centered, refusing-to-gt-under hoodlum and totally hedonistic. At one point, Bogart remarks that the only thing Robinson has ever wanted is *more!* And Robinson is pleased to hear it, even though it was meant as an insult. And he says, 'That's right. That's what I want. More!' Then, his treatment of Claire Trevor when she's begging for the drink, and he promises her one if she'll sing, is satanic in that he refuses her when she's finished, by saying that she didn't do a very good job of singing. He's sadistic, brutal, and at the same time very satanic, and at the end pathetic."

3. BARRY SULLIVAN in *The Gangster* (1947)
   "This is a small and neglected film. It's almost a lost one. It opens and ends with a satanic statement, and you know that the man, played by Sullivan, is doomed. This is not a Legs Diamond or an Al Capone story;

it's a psychological tale about a ganster who is perhaps too cultured and too sensitive and too kind to be a ruthless gangster. He has risen from the slums into the only role he could, into his destiny. Much like Lucifer, the fallen angel, he finds himself a victim of his circumstance. At the end, just before he's shot down in the rain, which is typical *film noir,* he's castigated by this young girl whose father wants to hide him. She refuses him refuge, and just before he plunges into the rain to his death, he delivers a bitter diatribe: his only sin was that he wasn't brutal enough to make a true success as a gangster; he wasn't cut out for it and didn't want it, but it was the only thing open to him; and he should've been more ruthless, because that's the way the world really is. It's a purely satanic soliloquy, of a victim in a role he should never have been thrust into.''

4. GEORGE SANDERS in *The Moon and Sixpence* (1942)
   "Sanders was a satanist par excellence in practically everything he did, but this is a standout. And coupled with his role in *The Picture of Dorian Gray* (1945), he has created some of the most satanic images of all time, simultaneously evil and sophisticated.''

5. WALTER HUSTON in *The Treasure of the Sierra Madre* (1948)
   "Of course, Huston did a memorable job as Scratch in *All That Money Can Buy* (1941), but his most satanic role was in *Sierra Madre,* where

In one of the most satanic screen portrayals ever, Edward G. Robinson menaces Humphrey Bogart in *Key Largo* (1948).

he was the only one who came out unscathed. He was the old geezer who knew the score, who was nobody's fool when it came down to survival, rather than the doddering old coot they expected. He was the one who got the last laugh, and got the entire Mexican militia laughing as the bags of gold were scattered by the wind. He saw the supreme irony. He'd warned Dobbs, Bogart's character, about becoming over-whelmed by greed, but Dobbs said it wouldn't happen to him. Yet it did. Huston's character knew what evil lurks in the hearts of men—to coin a phrase.''

6. VINCENT PRICE as *The Abominable Dr. Phibes* (1971)

"With all the roles you'd expect him to have, only two are standout satanic portrayals: *The Abominable Dr. Phibes* (1971) and its sequel, *Dr. Phibes Rises Again* (1972). In these, he pulled out all the stops and created a camped-up essence of satanic characterization. His *The Masque of the Red Death* (1964) is also memorable.''

7. FREAKS (1932)

"This highly satanic (in the sense of dealing with disciples of Satan), bizarre little film by Tod Browning had to go underground for many years, even though it was produced at MGM as a sort of competitive film for Universal's *Frankenstein*. Browning used real freaks and mal-formed people, which disgusted not only much of MGM but audiences as well. It's purely satanic in that audience sympathies lie with the freaks themselves, and the villains are the straight people, who are the cruel exploiters of human misery. You cheer at the end when the freaks rise up and turn their keeper into one of them.''

8. PETER COOKE in *Bedazzled* (1967)

"Raquel Welch played a small but important part, that of Lust, in this updating of the Faust legend. Cook plays Lucifer, with humor and style, and so convincingly that the audience wonders how such a personable young man could be the Devil.''

9. PETER O'TOOLE in *The Ruling Class* (1972)

"This is an oddball film that they tried to sell as a comedy, but it's really a tragedy with comedy overtones. O'Toole's transition in the film starts with him being quite naive, a total innocent, and takes him to the bru-talizing total cynic at the end, when diabolically, he takes on the role of the devil incarnate. He starts the film thinking he's Jesus Christ, but he's very anti-Christ because he's blasphemous despite himself. And, of course, everyone thinks him insane. Then as he transcends, or descends, from the Christ-identification to thinking he's Jack the Ripper, he finds that people more readily accept him, and rejoice that he's not cured of his insanity. He's normal now that he's a real rotten son-of-a-bitch who dresses in black, advocates torture, and kills people. At the end there's that blasphemous scene where he's leading the decaying corpses singing 'Onward Christian Soldiers.' ''

10. ERNEST BORGNINE in *The Devil's Rain* (1975)

"Borgnine's done some marvelous satanic portrayals, but his most out-standing was this one. His visage as the goat, his overbearing arrogance, his proud stance, and final victory were great. The director, Robert Fuest, who'd done such a neat job with *Dr. Phibes,* really had no concept of what this picture was all about, and it was really Borgnine's demonic personification that saved it. He gave the role, and the picture, power and stature."

... AND 10 HONORABLE MENTIONS

1. NILS ASTER in *The Bitter Tea of General Yen* (1933)
2. CHARLES BRONSON in *Death Wish* (1974)
3. SIDNEY BLACKMER in *Rosemary's Baby* (1968)
4. BORIS KARLOFF in *The Black Cat* (1934)
5. CHARLES LAUGHTON in *The Island of Lost Souls* (1933)
6. ALISTAIR SIM in *An Inspector Calls* (1954)
7. SAM JAFFE in *The Asphalt Jungle* (1950)
8. CLAUDE RAINS in *The Invisible Man* (1933)
9. FREDRIC MARCH in *Dr. Jekyll and Mr. Hyde* (1931)
10. BURGESS MEREDITH in *The Torture Garden* (1967)

ANTON LA VEY'S LIST OF 3 OF MARILYN MONROE'S ATTRIBUTES WHICH IRONICALLY LED TO HER EVOLVEMENT INTO THE SUPREME SEX GODDESS

Says La Vey: "Marilyn and I met in September of 1948 when I was the organist at the Mayan Theatre on Hill Street in Los Angeles. It was a burlesque house, and she was a stripper. Not a headliner, just filling in for a few weeks because she was hungry. She'd just been let go by 20th Century-Fox, which didn't renew her contract. She was just another blonde starlet in a town full of blonde starlets. Her only film credits had been two minor roles in *Ladies of the Chorus* and *Dangerous Years;* and she was on the rebound from an affair with a musical director at Fox. But mostly she didn't know where her next job was coming from, so she took off her clothes at the burlesque house and also did some nude modeling. It was a very lean period for her.

"We met and hit it off, and saw a lot of each other in the next few months. She was living at the Hollywood Studio Club at the time, and she didn't want them to know what she was doing, so she took

a little place on Washington Boulevard. And I lived with her for a short time. It was a cardboard carton and shoe box arrangement. I was a drifter then and so it was ideal for me. She was fascinated with the dark side of life, about the occult and death, and didn't have a frivolity about her as you might imagine. She had this battered old car that we used to drive down to the beach. I remember she drove me to the draft board to register for the draft for the Korean War.

"I had never cared for blondes before then, but there was something special about her. But I was only eighteen, even though I made out like I was twenty-five, and I was rather opportunistic. Before too long I got involved with a woman who had a lot of money, and Marilyn and I stopped seeing each other. We kept in touch for a year or two; I did get letters from her occasionally. And you can't help but think over the years, 'What if. . . ? What if I had been more persistent and less of a drifter?' But as is characteristic of youth, I fancied myself much more callous and worldly than I really was.

"The great irony about Marilyn was not that it took so long for her special qualities to be recognized, but that she became a sex symbol at all. True, she evoked an emotional response from people, much in the way that James Dean or Elvis did. There was this charisma about her, but her basic qualifications, if you can call them that, were all wrong.

1. "Marilyn was a deviation from the physical type that was in vogue in the early fifties. She was much too voluptuous in an era when the top leading ladies were thin and gamine. She seemed to be always concerned about her weight, especially after Harry Cohn at Columbia had referred to her as a 'fat cow.' Yet, he tried to arrange clandestine rendezvous with her, which only heightened the paradox of her sexuality.
2. "No matter how she was dressed, when she moved, Marilyn always gave you the impression that she was about to expose herself. Rather than looking like she was poured into her clothes, she always looked like she was about to fall out of them. She didn't dress like that on purpose. It was rather because of her proportions, the length of her arms and legs, and the way she was put together. And because of it she appeared to be a little untidy.
3. "A lot has been said about her vulnerability and sense of naiveté, but what it really was, was that she looked so approachable. She had an easy look, a common look that held her down because she seemed so attainable. Marilyn was the kind of woman that men desired, but not to take home to mother. And the intrinsic paradox here was that if, in your fantasy, you did attain her, you would then become intimidated by her.

ilyn Monroe in the most famous calendar pose of all time. While trying to k into movies, she did some nude modeling because "I was hungry."

"The greatest irony about her, as is the case too often with people with uniquely special qualities, is that it wasn't until after her death that she was finally truly appreciated. And her legend took on mythic proportions. If she had lived . . . who knows?"

PETER HARRISON ELLENSHAW'S LIST OF 4 SCIENCE FICTION MOVIES THAT REVOLUTIONIZED SPECIAL EFFECTS

Peter Harrison Ellenshaw is the son of Peter Ellenshaw, one of the major pioneers in the field of special and visual effects, who won an Oscar for his innovative work on *Mary Poppins* (1964). The younger Ellenshaw, following in his father's footsteps, has made major contributions to the special effects on such films as *The Man Who Fell to Earth* (1976), *Star Wars* (1977), *The Black Hole* (1979), and *The Empire Strikes Back!* (1980), among others.

Gary Lockwood and Keir Dullea in Stanley Kubrick's *2001: A Space Odyssey* (1968), which made space hardware a tangible reality. No science fiction film has ever been the same since.

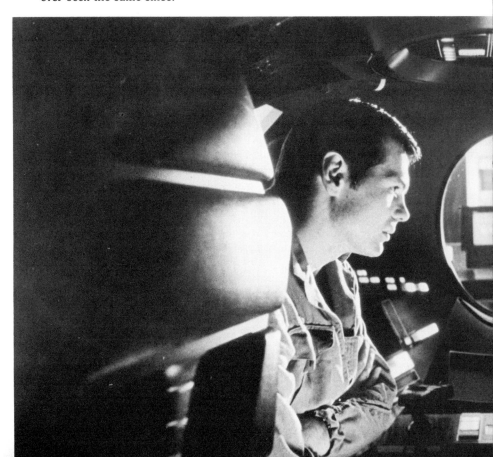

1. THINGS TO COME (1936)
   Director: William Cameron Menzies; Raymond Massey, Cedric Hardwicke. "My dad worked on this one and it shows how much of an innovator he was. There was extensive model work, used more effectively and realistically than they had before. He created extensive miniatures and painted matte backgrounds that gave the small sets a feeling of bigness. The visual effects gave the picture a great deal of scope. Much of it was rudimentary by today's standards, but this picture opened the way for such films as *Destination Moon* (1950) and *When Worlds Collide* (1951)."

2. 2001: A SPACE ODYSSEY (1968)
   D: Stanley Kubrick; Keir Dullea, Gary Lockwood. Special Effects by Kubrick. "This was a real trend-setter, and broke new ground. The whole film was based on its special effects. It was a monumental achievement, and made space hardware a tangible reality for the first time. No science fiction film has ever been the same since then."

3. STAR WARS (1977)

   D: George Lucas; Mark Hamill, Carrie Fisher, Harrison Ford. Special Effects by John Dykstra. "This is the result of the vision of one man, George Lucas. He packed this film with so much visual excitement. The tremendous number of effects created an environment for the story. Speeding spaceships and laser blasts became a new staple of science fiction films."

4. ALIEN (1979)

   D: Ridley Scott; Tom Skeritt, Sigourney Weaver, John Hurt. "The visual effects by Brian Johnson and Nick Alider were exceptionally low key, which is what made them work so well. They created a future world that wasn't antiseptic and deodorized and sterile, but rather lived in and used every day. This was the first genuinely successful blend of horror with science fiction."

11

CHAPTER

HOW THE WEST WAS WON

Or: *Sometimes the Hero Kisses His Horse*

REX ALLEN'S LIST OF THE TOP 10 WESTERN STARS OF ALL TIME

One of the last and most successful stars to appear in a series of B-Westerns, Rex Allen began his motion picture career in *Arizona Cowboy* (1949). Already an established country singer, he fit easily into the mold of the singing cowboy begun by Gene Autry some fifteen years before. Allen's films were superior to most of the matinée Westerns of the day: they were often in color, featured good supporting casts, attractive leading ladies for romantic interludes (which usually revolved around a musical number), and the scripts were better than average. Quickly overshadowing well-established stars like Rocky Lane, Monte Hale, Lash LaRue, and others, Allen became the number two cowpoke on the Republic lot, second only to Roy Rogers, the reigning King of the Cowboys. When Roy finally left the Republic corral for television, Rex became the top cinema sagebrush hero, and remained so until 1954, when the era of the B-Western ended. His final theatrical was *The Phantom Stallion*.

Rex Allen knows his Western stars. He's one of the permanent trustees of the Cowboy Hall of Fame in Oklahoma City, Oklahoma.

1. TOM MIX (1880–1940)

"He was the best of the early cowboy stars, who did his own stunts and even directed himself. He was the beginning of the Western hero who wore flashy clothes and had some theatrics about him. He even had his own Wild West show and circus. Mix had been one of Teddy Roosevelt's Rough Riders during the Spanish-American War; he'd also been a Texas Ranger, an Indian scout, a rodeo champion, and the first all-around cowboy to become a Western movie hero. In 1918, he became a star in a series of silent Westerns, and went on to make over 400 pictures. That's a record. And he was the first cowboy to make his horse a star—Tony, the wonder horse of the movies, who outlived him by four years. Mix died in 1940 in an automobile accident. It made the front page of my local paper in Willcox, Arizona. I was in my last year in high school."

2. BUCK JONES (1894–1942)

"He and Mix were the best of the bunch in the early thirties. Jones had been in the U.S. Cavalry and served in the Philippines; he was a rodeo performer and a Wild West show rider and trick roper before coming to Hollywood in 1917 to start making pictures. By 1920, he was a star. He and his champion horse, Silver, were big box office until the advent of the musical Western. He died in 1942 trying to save people in a nightclub fire. He was only forty-eight; a hero to the end."

3. HOOT GIBSON (1895–1962)

"He was a bona-fide world champion bronc rider before he was twenty, and toured the world with a Wild West show like Mix, Jones, and some of the others. His nickname 'Hoot' came from his hunting owls as a boy. After starting in pictures in 1915, he became Universal's top Western star. His films had a lot of humor and lots of action, mostly because he got his start in the business as a stuntman. He was called the 'Dean of Cowboy Action.' "

4. KEN MAYNARD (1895–1973)

"Here's another real cowboy who grew up in Texas and started in the silent days. He was one of the best stunt riders on the screen, and had a beautiful trick horse named Tarzan. He was one of your better-looking cowboys, so he got to kiss the girl every once in a while."

5. TIM McCOY (1891–1978)

"Colonel Tim McCoy started in pictures in 1923 when he came to Hollywood as adviser on *The Covered Wagon,* being an ex-Cavalry officer and all. His rank of Colonel sort of stuck with him, perhaps because he was a military kind of actor, sort of stiff, a kind of cowboy MacArthur. He made some eighty-nine pictures, and was the world's foremost authority on Indian sign language. He studied it all his life, taught it, and worked with the Indians in my home state for his last twenty years."

estern star Rex Allen mounts his famous horse Koko to ride to stardom in *izona Cowboy* (1949). He became the most popular sagebrush hero of the 50s, second only to Roy Rogers.

6. BEN JOHNSON (1919–   )

"Along with Hoot Gibson, Ben's the only bona-fide champion cowboy to make a name for himself in pictures. He won the world champion steer roping in 1953, so he qualifies on this list, even though he's not what you'd call a Western star of a series of films. But just look at his credits: *Three Godfathers* (1949), *She Wore a Yellow Ribbon* (1949), *Wagonmaster* (1950), *Rio Grande* (1950), *Shane* (1953) . . . yeah, he qualifies; I don't see how you can leave him off."

7. GENE AUTRY (1907–   )

"Gene popularized the singing cowboy role and became one of the most successful Westerners ever. He pioneered the musical Western in 1934 with *Tumblin' Tumbleweeds*. From 1937 to 1942, he was the top moneymaking movie cowboy. His popularity waned during his absence from the screen while serving with the Air Force in World War II. After the war, he went right back to it, and shot right up into the top ten again. This Texan was probably the most business-minded of all the Western stars, and his investments have done real well."

8. ROY ROGERS (1912–   )

"Roy started his career as Leonard Slye, a member of the Sons of the Pioneers singing group. He signed with Republic in 1937 as a singing cowboy, and within six years he was the undisputed King of the Cowboys. From 1943 to 1954 he was the number one moneymaking Western star. He was bigger than Autry, or John Wayne, or anybody else in the saddle. His appeal was that he was young, very handsome, had a good voice, was a fantastic entertainer, and the public was ready for him. He was a hard worker who went out and did it. I think he started out poor, and wanted to make good. He paid his dues and he damn well deserves everything good that's happened to him. He's just a fantastic individual, and I think a lot of him. I think he was a damn good actor, too, and so was Autry and a lot of these others . . . considering the material they had to work with."

9. JOHN WAYNE (1907–1979)

"There's nobody you can compare John Wayne to. He was in a class by himself, a legend. John was the number one Western hero of all time. Just in terms of longevity, there's nobody who can match him. In the thirties alone he made some forty-five B-Westerns before *Stagecoach* (1939) kicked off his career in major productions. So, while the rest of us did the programers, John made the epic Westerns, some of the best Western films ever made. He was a good actor, too, but he sang lousy. Not too many know that he was supposed to be the first singing cowboy on the screen. They tried him out as 'Singin' Sandy' in *Riders of Destiny,* predating Autry by a year. That was 1933, but as it turned out, it was one thing he couldn't do."

10. JOEL McCREA (1905–   )

Roy Rogers, the King of the Cowboys. In 1945, he became one of the top ten box-office stars and remained the number one movie Western hero for a decade until he left films to go into television.

"I can't say enough nice things about Joel. He's just an A-number-one beautiful man. He's a neighbor of mine, and we're both trustees on the Cowboy Hall of Fame in Oklahoma. He started in features about 1929, did a lot of bedroom pictures, but a lot of Westerns too; and then nothing but Westerns from the mid-forties on. He was the star of a lot of the bigger-budget color Westerns that replaced the B-Westerns after TV came in. His *Ride the High Country* (1962) is a genuine classic."

...and 3 OBVIOUS OMISSIONS

1. WILLIAM S. HART (1870–1946)
   "You might put him on the list but I wouldn't. He was a Shakespearean actor from the New York stage, who made a lot of bedroom pictures."
2. RANDOLPH SCOTT (1903–   )
   "He's not a cowboy in the first place. He's from Virginia, a former college boy and male model . . . a Southern cattleman type. He did a lot of Westerns . . . with a great big fat Southern accent, which didn't bother me none. Sure, Randolph Scott was very big, but I don't consider him a Western star."
3. CLINT EASTWOOD (1930–   )
   "He's in the modern end of it, and I don't think of him as a Western actor as such. How the hell are you going to put Clint Eastwood in the same category with Roy Rogers, Autry, and Mix. He doesn't fit. He's a spaghetti Westerner, talks dirty, hollers 's---' . . . he uses four-letter words, has gravy on his tie, and rapes somebody, well then he's a great hero. You want to know the truth. I don't like the kind of pictures he makes. That's not the way I see things."

Allen concludes: "I see the Western coming back. Maybe next year or the year after. Everyone's wearing cowboy clothes today, boots and hats. I've got some Western suits made for me in the fifties, and they look like I just got them. I've been wearing Western clothes for forty years and I'm finally in style.

"But Westerns have always been in style. When they wanted to rejuvenate a star, they'd stick him in a Western. They'd say, 'Alan Ladd is pooped out at the box office; let's put him in a Western and bring him back.' And they did. They did it with Errol Flynn, Fred MacMurray, James Stewart, even Wayne. That's cause a Western never lost money. They all made a profit. Put that down as a quote . . . no action Western ever lost money at the box office."

CLINT EASTWOOD'S 4 FAVORITE JOHN WAYNE FILMS

Clint Eastwood, the number one box-office draw in the world, who is himself truly underrated as an actor, feels that John Wayne was never given the true recognition he deserved as the fine actor he could be in the right role.

Claims Eastwood: "Duke was best in character parts, in roles where he had to stretch as an actor. The mistake he made in later years was that he should've evolved naturally into more character

John Wayne gave one his best character portrayals in *Red River* (1948), which also starred Joanne Dru, and introduced Montgomery Clift to the moviegoing public.

In *The Quiet Man*, shown here with Barry Fitzgerald, John Wayne proved he could act.

roles, like his wonderful portrayal in *True Grit*. The fact that he got an Oscar for that is proof that he could be very good. I feel it was a mistake for him to have tried to keep playing the hero. That's why some of his pictures didn't do business at the end. The public didn't buy it anymore. I think he was at his best in these four films":

1. RED RIVER (1948)
   "He was still a young man playing much older, and he was damn good. This is one of the all-time great Westerns." Director: Howard Hawks; Wayne, Montgomery Clift (in his film debut), Walter Brennan, Joanne Dru, John Ireland
2. THE QUIET MAN (1952)
   D: John Ford; Wayne, Maureen O'Hara, Victor McLaglen, Barry Fitzgerald, Ward Bond
3. THE SEARCHERS (1956)
   D: John Ford; Wayne, Jeffrey Hunter, Vera Miles (in her first major role), Ward Bond, Natalie Wood
4. TRUE GRIT (1969)
   D: Henry Hathaway; Wayne, Kim Darby, Glen Campbell

BOB MUNDEN'S LIST OF THE 5 QUICKEST DRAWS IN HOLLYWOOD

In the *Guinness Book of World Records,* Bob Munden is listed as the fastest-moving human being in the world. He can draw and fire a six-gun faster than anyone ever in the history of the world! His time to clear leather, cock, and fire his pistol is an incomprehensible 2/100ths of a second. In a mind-stopping demonstration, he can draw and fire twice so fast that to the eyes and ears it appears that he has only fired once; yet two targets in two different locations are shattered! He is the ultimate Mr. Lightning!

At thirty-eight years old, Munden, who's been competing for twenty-seven years, has won over 3,500 trophies, 522 major championships, and has held all the world speed records in the fast draw for two decades. He is the only full-time shooting exhibitionist in the world—except for his wife, Becky, who is the world record holder in the women's division.

Munden says: "The fast draw was created by the movies. There's no historical fact to substantiate it at all. It's all fiction. It's really a modern-day sport and highly sophisticated. The draw is measured by an electronic timer, which starts with the draw and is stopped automatically by the sound of the gunfire. It can measure an increment of time as minute as 3/1,000ths of a second."

Over the years, Munden has had an opportunity to personally test and to observe some of Hollywood's finest go for their guns. Though none can touch his speed, they are speed artists in their own right.

1. JERRY LEWIS (35/100ths of a second)
   "He became interested in it, and had a natural ability."
2. SAMMY DAVIS, JR. (40/100ths of a second)
   "I ran into him in a gun store and ended up working with him and testing him at home."
3. CLINT EASTWOOD (45/100ths of a second)
   "He's the only celebrity who has actually fired in a tournament and done this well."
4. GLENN FORD (45–50/100ths of a second)
5. AUDIE MURPHY (50/100ths of a second)
   "He was a very competitive guy and had a standing challenge to all movie stars, anytime, anyplace—only he wanted to use real bullets."

Munden adds: "When Hugh O'Brien was hot on TV in 'Wyatt Earp,' he fancied himself a quick-draw man. But he wasn't even as fast as these guys, and was actually beaten several times."

THE GENE AUTRY 10-POINT COWBOY CODE (CIRCA 1950)

1. A cowboy never takes unfair advantage—even of an enemy
2. A cowboy never betrays a trust
3. A cowboy always tells the truth
4. A cowboy is kind to small children, to old folks, and to animals
5. A cowboy is free from racial and religious prejudice
6. A cowboy is helpful and, when anyone's in trouble, he lends a hand
7. A cowboy is a good worker
8. A cowboy is clean about his person and in thought, word, and deed
9. A cowboy respects womanhood, his parents, and the laws of his country
10. A cowboy is a patriot

Autry himself is said to have written the above code, and though it seems dated and somewhat hokey today, there's a wistful nostalgia about it and the old-fashioned values it expresses. If only it were possible for all of us to be "cowboys" and to live by the code. Damn! Wouldn't it be something?!

A Fawcett Publication

LASH LARUE
WESTERN

OCT.
10¢
NO. 21

IN THIS ISSUE:
*THE FRONTIER
PHANTOM
RIDES AGAIN.*

Living by the Cowboy Code was obviously the right thing for Autry to do. Because as his longtime movie sidekick, Pat Buttram, observed: "For three decades Gene used to ride off into the sunset—now he owns it."

LASH LaRUE'S LIST OF A HALF-DOZEN CINEMA COWPOKES WITH A GIMMICK

Al "Lash" LaRue was, in all honesty, the most unlikely Western hero ever to chew up the cinema sagebrush. He wasn't particularly tall, nor exceptionally well built, nor a singer, nor even good-looking; in fact, he looked villainous and surly, the kind of man you wouldn't buy a used car from. And he always wore black, from his flat crown Stetson to his boots; plus, he wasn't much of a horseman. Yet he shot to popularity in the late 1940s and overshadowed many more personable and appealing Western stars. Sure, he had a gimmick (that twelve-foot black bullwhip from which his screen handle was derived) but so did a lot of other cowboys.

Lash said: "You know, there were a lot of cowboys in the heyday of B-Westerns in the forties and fifties, and to stand out, you had to have something special, something that set you out from the rest of the straight-shooters. I got my start as a villain called the Cheyenne Kid in an Eddie Dean picture—remember him? I wore all black and tried to scare a widow off her ranch. I was real bad, but toward the end of the picture I found out that I was her long-lost son and that made me go straight. I looked kinda surly and unappealing, yet I got a ton of mail for that picture and it led to my own series of films, first as the Cheyenne Kid, and then as Lash LaRue, when I started using a bullwhip. The whip became my trademark, my gimmick—that and my all-black outfit. I was the first hero who looked like the villain."

1. LASH LaRUE
   "My gimmick was pretty good. It worked for quite a few years. I still get mail."
2. WHIP WILSON
   "Here was a guy who could really use a whip. He was a rodeo rider turned actor, and all his pictures were just excuses for him to show off what he could do with that whip."
3. WILD BILL ELLIOTT
   "He wore his guns backward. Nobody could figure out how he drew

Al "Lash" LaRue was the unlikeliest cowpoke ever to gallop across the silver screen. He wore black and hated horses. But he had a surefire gimmick: his twelve-foot black bullwhip.

them so fast, wearing them that way. He called it a cross-draw. Rex Allen, later, wore them the same way."
4. BILL BOYD (as Hopalong Cassidy)
   "He was the first guy to sport all-black clothes, but he rode a pure white horse and had a head of white hair."
5. CLAYTON MOORE (as the Lone Ranger)
   "What can you say about the Lone Ranger that everybody doesn't already know?"
6. CHARLES STARRETT
   "He wore a mask, and had an all-black outfit, too, and called himself the Durango Kid."

LaRue, like many actors, has had his bouts with liquor and drugs; after a lifetime of flirting with religion, he's joined a monastery in St. Petersburg, Florida.

THE TOP 10 WESTERN STARS AT THE BOX OFFICE IN ENGLAND IN 1952

1. JOHN WAYNE
2. ALAN LADD
3. RANDOLPH SCOTT
4. ROY ROGERS
5. JAMES STEWART
6. JOEL McCREA
7. GENE AUTRY
8. REX ALLEN
9. BURT LANCASTER
10. ERROL FLYNN

JOHN RITTER'S 6 FAVORITE CHILDHOOD WESTERN HEROES

Ritter, star of ABC-TV's hit series "Three's Company" (1977–present), grew up in a home steeped in Western lore. He is the son of the late great singing cowboy hero Tex Ritter, who appeared in over eighty Westerns during a screen career that spanned three decades.

Says Ritter, who in 1980 emceed a TV special about Western film heroes: "I grew up on Westerns and just love them. For a long time, I didn't know they made any other kind of pictures."

His favorite heroes in his formative years included:

1. TEX RITTER (naturally)
2. JOHN WAYNE
3. ROY ROGERS
4. RORY CALHOUN
5. TIM HOLT
6. HOOT GIBSON

TEX RITTER

A Fawcett Publication

WESTERN

APR.
10¢
NO. 10

DANGER AND DEATH ARE SADDLE MATES
WHEN TEX RITTER RIDES INTO
"THE GHOST TOWN!"

Western hero Tex Ritter made over eighty films in a career that spanned three decades and was an accomplished singer and musician. His son, John, stars on ABC-TV's "Three's Company."

5 THINGS THE NEW MOVIE LONE RANGER BECAME FAMOUS FOR DURING LOCATION FILMING OF *THE LEGEND OF THE LONE RANGER* IN SANTA FE, NEW MEXICO

Klinton Spilsbury, twenty-five, a nice-looking young man who'd had only two acting jobs before (both minor TV episodic roles) was somehow chosen to play the new Lone Ranger. He earned himself quite a reputation offscreen during location shooting in Santa Fe. According to eyewitness reports, news reporters, and the regulars at several local bars, Spilsbury gave new dimension to the Code of the West by:

1. Slapping a waitress across the face.
2. Falling down, spilling drinks, busting glasses, and trying to play piano with the house band.
3. Pounding on the bar, tossing drinks across the room, and explaining his heroic behavior by yelling: "Hey, I'm the Lone Ranger!"
4. Having difficulty mounting a horse and reciting lines.
5. Causing extras to walk off the set because they got tired of filming the same lines thirteen times.

Actor Clayton Moore, whose face has not been photographed since his identification with the role of the Lone Ranger began in 1949, was passed over for the new film, in favor of Spilsbury. Moore, in fact, has been sued by the Wrather Corporation (which owns the Lone Ranger character) to prevent him from making any future appearances in the famous black mask. Moore now makes personal appearances in wraparound black sunglasses, and had this to say: "They offered me a bit part in the movie, and they said they'd let me wear the mask again if I'd go out on the road and promote the movie. But there's no way Clayton Moore will do anything for this movie. I sure want no part of it, not after the shocking behavior by the young fellow who has the starring role. I just can't endure the thought of anybody damaging the image of such a great person as the Lone Ranger."

4 REASONS WHY *THE LEGEND OF THE LONE RANGER* WAS SHELVED

As of this writing, the new Lone Ranger film, which had been scheduled for a nationwide release for Christmas 1980, has been shelved temporarily (?). How temporarily only time will tell. Some pictures like Robert Altman's *M*A*S*H* and *Health* both gathered dust for a year

Clayton Moore, the man most identified with the role of the Lone Ranger, was offered a small part in the new movie based on the character, but turned it down because of the "shocking behavior" of the young actor now wearing the mask. (With Moore is the late Indian actor, Jay Silverheels, as Tonto.)

before they were distributed for fear that they would die at the box office. *M*A*S*H* didn't, of course, but *Health* did; as it is expected that *The Legend of the Lone Ranger* will. "From what I've gathered, it's the biggest stiff of the century," a major Chicago theatre owner has declared.

1. THE OFFICIAL REASON

   According to the Wrather Corporation, which owns the Lone Ranger character, the postponement is due to production delays. "The movie needs a little more post-production work before it will be ready for release."

2. THE CREATIVE REASON

   Some insiders have called the picture a 100-megaton bomb, and, reportedly, very few theatres were willing to risk the lucrative Christmas period with it, remembering the beating they took in 1976 with the remake of *King Kong*.

3. THE PUBLIC RELATIONS REASON ˙

   The film's young and inexperienced star, Klinton Spilsbury, managed to get some very damaging press during the production. Perhaps some distance (several years maybe) will give the public time to forget his indiscretions and after-hours imbroglios in local taverns on location in Santa Fe.

4. THE PUBLIC SENTIMENT REASON

   Reportedly, many potential moviegoers are angry about the shabby treatment of Clayton Moore, the man who had portrayed the Lone Ranger for so long, and who, in the public sentiment, is still the embodiment of that character.

12

CHAPTER

ALL THE PRESIDENT'S MEN

Or: *How Politics Are Just a French Kiss Removed from Showbiz*

10 REASONS WHY RONALD REAGAN'S FILM CAREER CRASHED

Following World War II, Reagan's film career waned. He had peaked with *King's Row* (1941), at which time, Warner Brothers publicity claimed, his fan mail was second only to Errol Flynn's. Here are some of his stepping stones to filmdom oblivion:

1. THAT HAGEN GIRL (1947)
   Shirley Temple is confused into thinking that she's Reagan's illegitimate daughter.
2. STALLION ROAD (1947)
   Reagan is a horse doctor wooing lady rancher Alexis Smith by tending her animals. The horses had the best lines.
3. NIGHT UNTO NIGHT (1949)
   Incredulous romance between dying scientist Reagan and mentally ill widow Viveca Lindfors.
4. BEDTIME FOR BONZO (1951)
   Professor Reagan treats a chimp as his child for an heredity experiment. Bonzo had the best lines.
5. THE LAST OUTPOST (1951)
   Brothers Reagan and Bruce Bennett are pitted against each other for Rhonda Fleming and the fate of the West. Indians add to the confusion.

Ronald Reagan suffers the demise of his film career at the hairy paws of Bonzo, who had the title role in *Bedtime for Bonzo* (1951).

6. SHE'S WORKING HER WAY THROUGH COLLEGE (1952)
   Burlesque queen Virginia Mayo gets the urge to—yup—go back to college. Reagan is best friend.
7. TROPIC ZONE (1953)
   Reagan fights to save Rhonda Fleming's banana plantation from an unscrupulous shipping magnate.
8. CATTLE QUEEN OF MONTANA (1954)
   Reagan fights to save Barbara Stanwyck's cattle ranch from unscrupulous land-grabbers.
9. TENNESSEE'S PARTNER (1955)
   John Payne as an unusual Western "heel," and Reagan accidentally becomes his best friend.
10. HELLCATS OF THE NAVY (1957)
   So-so Navy drama had Reagan fighting to save his career from unscrupulous box-office returns. (He lost.)

Reagan made one additional film, *The Killers* (1964), in which he made an impressive showing in a supporting villainous role. But to no avail, as, two years later, he lost a plum role in *Blindfold* to Dean Stockwell. And while the picture was in production, he announced his candidacy for governor of California.

When hearing about Reagan's candidacy, Jack Warner, Reagan's former boss at Warner Brothers, reportedly said: "No, no, no, no. It's all wrong. Jimmy Stewart for governor. Ronald Reagan for best friend."

10 CELEBRITY ONE-LINERS ABOUT RONALD REAGAN AS PRESIDENT

Jokes about an actor in the White House are inevitable. Robert Stack recalls the days when Ronald Reagan was the president of SAG: "After a board meeting one night, I told Ronnie that he should get into politics, that I'd vote for him if he ran for president. It got a big laugh." Well, today Reagan's still getting laughs.

1. JOHNNY CARSON
   "Reagan's first move toward balancing the national budget was to have the Voyager I's photos of Saturn developed at Fotomat."
2. CAROL CHANNING
   "Reagan wanted to be inaugurated for one week in December so that he'd be eligible for an Oscar this year."
3. JOHNNY CARSON
   "Have you seen the pictures in the news of Ronald Reagan vacationing

at his ranch, riding horseback—and George Bush following on foot with the pooper scooper?"

4. BOB SOLO
   "Reagan finally got what he wanted—a house with a projection room."

5. JOHNNY CARSON
   "One of his first official acts will be to repay an old friend, Liz Taylor. He's going to make her a state."

6. BOB HOPE
   "Ronnie promised Frank Sinatra he could be ambassador to Italy—but I don't know if they can stand two popes . . ."

7. JOHNNY CARSON
   "Have you seen the new presidential limousine? The license plate says 'Gipper One.' "

8. GEORGIE JESSEL
   "It's good to be with a winner—the last one I had was Seabiscuit."

9. JOHNNY CARSON
   "Reagan's in the news again. He's at his ranch chopping wood—he's building the log cabin he was born in."

10. BILL DANA
    "Maybe Reagan's been around for so long because Alpo's been around for so long."

13 SHOWBIZ FIGURES TO BECOME INVOLVED IN POLITICS

Though the connection between the two has always been rather ephemeral, show business and politics could both have been invented by P. T. Barnum. Both smack of the same drum beating puffery and are peopled with fantasy purveyors.

Now with Ronald Reagan in the White House, holding the highest political office in the country, the bond between show biz and politics is more tangible. Reagan, of course, is far from being the first entertainer to make that crossover.

1. GEORGE MURPHY, U.S. Senator from California
   He played Reagan's father in the 1942 Warner Brothers' musical, *This Is the Army.* A hoofer of some renown, Murphy began in films in the early 1930s; he made some forty pictures and won a Special Oscar in 1940, before leaving Hollywood in the 1950s for the U.S. Senate.

2. SHIRLEY TEMPLE BLACK, U.S. Ambassador to Ghana, and the U.N.
   She was the greatest child star in the history of motion pictures. A genuine prodigy, she began dancing and singing her way to stardom at age three in 1931. Her simple optimism and cheery outlook helped America

In this 1935 photo, Shirley Temple assumes a napoleonic pose, perhaps for telling her future entrance into political life.

through the doldrums of the Depression. She costarred with George Murphy in *Little Miss Broadway* (1938) and played Reagan's stepdaughter in *That Hagen Girl* (1947); and following a sixteen-year movie career, she did a TV series before going into California politics in the 1960s.

3. ROBERT MONTGOMERY, Advisor to President Eisenhower
He was a smooth leading man of the 1930s and 1940s, best remembered for *Here Comes Mr. Jordan* (1941), *The Lady in the Lake* (1946), and the "Robert Montgomery Presents" TV series.

4. MIKE CURB, California Lieutenant Governor
Former record industry executive, and leader of the Mike Curb Congregation singing group. He should've stayed in entertainment, because all he's succeeded in doing in politics is displaying his bad judgment and misuse of gubernatorial powers whenever governor Jerry Brown is out of the state. Curb needs to be kept on a leash.

5. JOHN LODGE, Governor of Connecticut
Lodge, an actor in the 1930s, was Marlene Dietrich's leading man in *The Scarlet Empress* (1934), and gave up acting for the bright lights of politics.

6. REX BELL, Lieutenant Governor of Nevada
Western star of the 1930s and 1940s; retired his spurs for the Nevada State Capitol building.

7. MELINA MERCOURI, Member of Greek Parliament
Greek actress who became an international star in *Never on Sunday* (1960) has since gone into government.

8. VANESSA REDGRAVE, Palestinian Supporter
The controversial actress has made an unsuccessful bid for a post in Parliament in England.

9. JIMMIE DAVIS, Governor of Louisiana
Country and Western singer who, when elected to office, took some members of his musical group into politics with him.

10. CLAIRE BOOTHE LUCE, U.S. Ambassador to Italy
Former actress and playwright who married multimillionaire Henry Luce and gained some political clout.

11. GRACE KELLY, Crown Princess of Monaco
In a modern-day version of the Cinderella legend, Oscar-winning actress Grace Kelly retired from the screen to marry Prince Rainier of Monaco, and became Her Serene Highness Princess Grace.

12. POPE JOHN PAUL II
Before turning to political and religious activism in the Catholic Church, the pontiff was an actor and playwright. And perhaps he should be on Dennis Weaver's list of celebrities who have a secret desire to be a successful singer because the Pope is also an accomplished folk singer and an album of his tunes was released (no kidding) in 1979.

13. EVA PERON, wife of Argentine Dictator Juan Peron

Perhaps the most powerful and most notorious of all showbiz figures in past political life was Eva Peron, who has been canonized in a fashion in 1980's highly successful and overly romanticized musical, "Evita." She was a well-known Argentinian film actress before marrying Peron; and became immensely powerful and greatly feared in her own right.

6 ACTRESSES LINKED ROMANTICALLY WITH JOHN F. KENNEDY

This is speculation, of course, but some names keep popping up insistently when former President John F. Kennedy's private life is discussed. He's reputed to have been quite a swinger. You could say that this is another of the ephemeral connections between showbiz and politics.

1. MARILYN MONROE

She's the most celebrated of the actresses said to have been involved with JFK. Although many thought that she was dating Robert Kennedy, he was just a decoy to mask her actual affair with the president. Her alleged suicide in 1962 has been attributed to the cooling of their year-long affair.
2. ANGIE DICKINSON

Before Burt Bacharach, there was JFK.
3. JAYNE MANSFIELD
4. GENE TIERNEY
5. JUDY CAMPBELL
6. MONIQUE VAN VOOREN

She has referred to JFK as a "stage door Johnny," having allegedly dated him when he was a Massachusetts Senator in 1953. And she was known as "The Belgian Bulge" because of her magnificent bust, which, when considered with the attributes of some of the others on this list, reveals something about the sexual preferences of the late president.

THE HOLLYWOOD TEN

By 1947, the anti-Communist hunt had cast a dark cloud over the movie colony.

The first celebrated casualties were the Hollywood Ten, a stalwart group of filmmakers, writers, directors, and producers, who refused to testify before the HUAC because they claimed it was unconstitutional. They were martyred; their careers ruined; some went into exile;

The chalkboard reads:

MEN'S WARDROBE

PIC. 783 DATE 10-2-

TITLE Do Re Mi

DIR. F. Tashlin

ACTOR Jayne Mansfield

PART OF Jerri

CHANGE #7

WORN Sc. 139-153

Murdocks Barbecue

Des. Le Maire

8 + 10

TESTED BY

Jayne Mansfield proudly displays her superstructure, which caught the eye of a lot of people, including the late John F. Kennedy.

Lana Turner and John Garfield in the *film noir* masterpiece, *The Postman Always Rings Twice* (1946). He was a smoldering talent with two Oscar nominations and the promise of a brilliant career ahead, when the McCarthy witch hunts ruined him.

some went to jail. It would be years before any of them would work in films again.

1. HERBERT BIBERMAN
2. ALBERT MALTZ
3. EDWARD DMYTRYK
4. ADRIAN SCOTT
5. RING LARDNER, JR.
6. SAMUEL ORNITZ
7. JOHN HOWARD LAWSON
8. LESTER COLE
9. ALVAH BESSIE
10. DALTON TRUMBO

... AND 10 OTHER CELEBRITIES WHO WERE BLACKLISTED

In addition to the Hollywood Ten, countless others were blacklisted and ostracized by the film world. They could not find work. Some eventually got back into the business after Kirk Douglas drove a wedge into the blacklist by openly hiring Dalton Trumbo to write the screenplay for *Spartacus* (1960).

1. LARRY PARKS
2. CHARLES CHAPLIN
3. JOHN GARFIELD
4. GALE SONDERGAARD
5. ANNE REVERE
6. DASHIEL HAMMETT
7. LILLIAN HELLMAN
8. LEE GRANT
9. LEE J. COBB
10. LIONEL STANDER
11. J. EDWARD BROMBERG

13 CHAPTER

THAT'S ENTERTAINMENT

Or: *Selected Subjects and Voices in the Dark*

JOHNNY WEISSMULLER'S 9 FAVORITE MOVIE TARZANS

Johnny Weissmuller, who catapulted to international fame in the title role of MGM's *Tarzan the Apeman* (1932), was an Olympic swimming champion with more gold medals and free-style records than anyone else. In 1950, he was named by the Associated Press National Poll as "the greatest swimmer of the past half century." He had been a scrawny, sickly kid who was told to take up swimming to combat the effects of a withering illness. Boy, did he learn to swim! And in the process he developed into a 6'3", 190-lb. world champion athlete, who, it seems, found his most enduring fame as Tarzan of the movies. Over a sixteen-year reign as king of the cinema jungle, he appeared in twelve Tarzan films and then went on to make twenty Jungle Jim films between 1948 and 1956, a role which he successfully transplanted to television.

Admitted Weissmuller: "You have to understand that it's difficult for me to think of anybody else as Tarzan. I did it for so long that most everybody thinks of me when you say Tarzan. And I'm sort of the same way. I think of me and Tarzan together. Even those Jungle Jim films I made were all just Tarzan with clothes on. But if I had to

The most famous Tarzan of the movies, Johnny Weissmuller, in *Tarzan and His Mate* (1934), with Paul Cavanaugh, Neil Hamilton, and Maureen O'Sullivan. O'Sullivan's costume as Jane was a sexy abbreviation until the new Production Code took affect, and in the following film she was slapped in leather from her shoulders to her knees.

list some of the other guys that played the character, I guess it'd go like this . . . after me'':

1. JOHNNY WEISSMULLER
    1932–48; 12 films as Tarzan
2. LEX BARKER
    1949–53; 5 films as Tarzan
3. BUSTER CRABBE
    1933; only film: *Tarzan the Fearless*
4. BRUCE BENNETT
    1935 serial, *New Adventures of Tarzan,* which was reissued in 1938 as a film, *Tarzan and the Green Goddess*

Weissmuller liked Gordon Scott personally and enjoyed him as Tarzan. Here, in a scene from *Tarzan's Hidden Jungle* (1955), he carries Vera Miles to safety.

5. JOCK MAHONEY
   1962–63; 2 films
6. GORDON SCOTT
   1955–60; 5 films
7. RON ELY
   1966–68; 2 seasons as the TV Tarzan; several 2-part episodes were edited into 2 feature films
8. DENNY MILLER
   1959; his film was the remake of Weissmuller's 1st movie, *Tarzan the Apeman.* "Denny's one helluva nice guy, but can you imagine—a blond Tarzan?"
9. JIM PIERCE
   1927's *Tarzan and the Golden Lion;* silent movie

NOTE: At this writing, Weissmuller, seventy-six, is barely alive in Acapulco, Mexico. A recent series of strokes has left him senile and bedridden. He is fed intravenously, inhales oxygen through tubes— and his devoted wife, Maria, is so distraught by his condition that she advocates euthanasia, a humane way of allowing him to die, rather than painfully prolonging his life.

ERNEST BORGNINE'S LIST OF 2 MOST MEMORABLE PORTRAYALS OF ABRAHAM LINCOLN ON THE SCREEN

Academy Award-winning movie villain and leading man, Borgnine reveals for the first time: "Not too many people know this, but I'm a Lincoln-phile. I've always admired him. Even as a boy, he was my ideal, a real homespun American hero. He was the greatest president there ever was. And in my home, I have a room containing Lincoln memorabilia and artifacts. It's my Lincoln Room, and the chief object is a painting of him done in the 1860s by M. M. Horn, a woman portrait painter. I bought it for $55 from a Bekins warehouse many years ago because I liked it. They were going to throw it out. Later, I discovered from a museum curator that it was a lost portrait worth anywhere from $500,000 to a million. It's my pride and joy. Someday I'm going to donate it to the National Archives for posterity.

"On film, there have been only two standout portrayals of Lincoln."

1. RAYMOND MASSEY in *Abe Lincoln in Illinois* (1940)
   "It was a tremendous picture, and I still can't figure why he didn't get an Oscar for it. He was wonderful. And, if you can believe it, he was asked

to do the part again twenty-three years later in *How the West Was Won.*
It was a small role, but a joy to see him as Lincoln again.''

2. HENRY FONDA in *Young Mr. Lincoln* (1939)
   "John Ford directed this, and it's some of Hank Fonda's best work ever.''

20 MOVIE AND REMAKE TITLES MATCHUP QUIZ

The old adage that there are only seven basic story plots was probably invented by a film producer who found it easier/safer (choose one) to do a new version of a successful picture than to develop a new one. Why take a chance when you can dust off an old chestnut and give it a fresh coat of paint—there, good as new—and pawn it off on the public, who'll buy it again, just as they did last time. Witness: Rex Beach's famous novel, *The Spoilers,* was filmed in 1914, 1923, 1930, 1942, and 1955.

Cecil B. DeMille was the first producer/director to film a remake. He was drawn back to his first film, *The Squaw Man* (1913), for a second version in 1918, the success of which prompted him to produce it a third time in 1931, this time as a talkie. He also remade his 1923 silent classic, *The Ten Commandments,* in 1956.

Somewhere along the line, a bright young producer came along and decided that what the old gray mare needed was not just a new hat, but a new name. Witness: *Three Blind Mice,* filmed in 1938 from the play by Stephen Powys, became *Moon over Miami* in 1941, and then *Three Little Girls in Blue* in 1946.

Moon Over Miami (1941), with Carole Landis, Robert Cummings, and Betty Grable, is only one of three movie versions of the play by Stephen Powys.

The next logical step was that if one of your seven basic plots works as a war film, of course it'll click as a Western, too. Or a desert epic. Witness: Bogart's combat classic *Sahara* (1943) was reincarnated as *Last of the Comanches* a decade later. Another timeless Bogart film, *To Have and Have Not* (1944), from the Ernest Hemingway novel, was translated (with many lines intact) into an Audie Murphy oater, *The Gun Runners,* in 1958.

The point of all this is that a remake is not always immediately identifiable as such. Here are twenty of these critters along with an earlier version of each for you to match up. (This is the third and final quiz, and the last chance to show your stuff.)

1. THE CHAMP (1931)
   Wallace Beery, Jackie Cooper
2. RED DUST (1932)
   Clark Gable, Jean Harlow
3. RAIN (1932)
   Joan Crawford, Walter Huston

4. IT HAPPENED ONE NIGHT (1934)
   Clark Gable, Claudette Colbert
5. SATAN MET A LADY (1936)
   Bette Davis, Warren William
6. ROMEO & JULIET (1936)
   Norma Shearer, Leslie Howard
7. PYGMALIAN (1938)
   Leslie Howard, Wendy Hiller

8. GUNGA DIN (1939)
   Cary Grant, Victor McLaglen
9. DARK VICTORY (1939)
   Bette Davis, George Brent
10. THE PHILADELPHIA STORY (1940)
    Katharine Hepburn, Cary Grant
11. HIS GIRL FRIDAY (1940)
    Cary Grant, Rosalind Russell

12. ROSE OF WASHINGTON SQUARE (1939)
    Alice Faye, Tyrone Power

a. CABARET (1972)
   Liza Minnelli, Michael York
b. THE CLOWN (1953)
   Red Skelton, Tim Considine
c. FAREWELL, MY LOVELY (1975)
   Robert Mitchum, John Ireland
d. THE FRONT PAGE (1974)
   Jack Lemmon, Walter Matthau

e. FUNNY GIRL (1968)
   Barbra Streisand, Omar Sharif
f. HEAVEN CAN WAIT (1978)
   Warren Beatty, Julie Christie
g. HELLO, DOLLY (1969)
   Barbra Streisand, Walter Matthau
h. HIGH SOCIETY (1956)
   Grace Kelly, Bing Crosby
i. LITTLE MISS MARKER (1980)
   Walter Matthau
j. THE MALTESE FALCON (1941)
   Humphrey Bogart, Mary Astor
k. THE MAGNIFICENT SEVEN (1960)
   Yul Brynner, Steve McQueen
l. MISS SADIE THOMPSON (1953)
   Rita Hayworth, Jose Ferrer

13. HERE COMES MR. JORDAN (1941)
    Robert Montgomery, Evelyn Keyes
14. MURDER, MY SWEET (1944)
    Dick Powell, Claire Trevor
15. SORROWFUL JONES (1949)
    Bob Hope, Lucille Ball
16. KISS ME KATE (1953)
    Howard Keel, Kathryn Grayson
17. THE SEVEN SAMURAI (1954)
    Toshiro Mifune
18. I AM A CAMERA (1955)
    Julie Harris, Laurence Harvey
19. THE MATCHMAKER (1958)
    Shirley Booth, Tony Perkins
20. THE LAST MAN ON EARTH (1964)
    Vincent Price

m. MOGAMBO (1953)
   Clark Gable, Ava Gardner
n. MY FAIR LADY (1964)
   Rex Harrison, Audrey Hepburn
o. THE OMEGA MAN (1971)
   Charlton Heston, Anthony Zerbe
p. SERGEANTS THREE (1962)
   Dean Martin, Frank Sinatra
q. STOLEN HOURS (1963)
   Susan Hayward, Michael Craig
r. TAMING OF THE SHREW (1967)
   Richard Burton, Liz Taylor
s. WEST SIDE STORY (1961)
   Natalie Wood, Richard Beymer
t. YOU CAN'T RUN AWAY FROM IT
   Jack Lemmon, June Allyson (1956)

ANSWERS

1. b, 2. m, 3. l, 4. t, 5. j, 6. s, 7. n, 8. p, 9. q, 10. h, 11. d, 12. e, 13. f, 14. c, 15. i, 16. r, 17. k, 18. a, 19. g, 20. o

MEL BLANC'S LIST OF 14 OF HIS FAVORITE CARTOON VOICES

In much the same way that Lon Chaney, Sr. was known as the man with a thousand faces, Mel Blanc is known as the man with a thousand voices. He got his first job at Warner Brothers in the late 1930s, when he demonstrated his unique talents by creating a voice for a drunken bull. Since then he's created hundreds of voices for characters we know and love, and hundreds of sound effects. He's said to have the vocal musculature of Enrico Caruso.

States Blanc: "I've always gotten a kick out of creating a voice for a cartoon character and bringing him to life. Over the years, I've done the voices for over 3,000 cartoons. The cartoons all seem to run together, but you remember the characters—they stay with you."

1. PORKY PIG

   "In one of my first sessions at Warners, Leon Schlesinger said, 'Hey, I got a pig that is a timid little character. Can you create a voice for him? His name is Porky Pig.' I thought about it, and said, 'If a pig could talk, he would talk with a grunt' . . . which developed into a stutter, and that's how Porky got his voice."

2. BUGS BUNNY

   "About Bugs, they said, 'He's a tough little character and a real stinker.' So I thought, 'Where in the country do the toughest voices come from?' Brooklyn, of course, and the Bronx. 'So, I put da two a dem together, doc,' and that's how Bugs got his voice. I also suggested that they call him Bugs Bunny after Bugs Hardaway, the guy who created him, instead of Happy Rabbit like they were going to."

3. TWEETY BIRD

   "Tweety was a baby bird, so I gave him a baby voice. 'Oooohh! I tawt I taw a putty tat.' "

4. SYLVESTER CAT

   "Sylvester's a big sloppy cat, so I gave him a big sloppy voice: 'Sthufferin' sthuckastash! You bet you sthaw a putty tat.' "

5. DAFFY DUCK

   "Daffy's voice is much like Sylvester's, only speeded up."

6. YOSEMITE SAM

   "Sam's voice is one of the toughest for me to do; it's tough on my throat. He's a little feisty character with a *great big voice!*"

7. FOGHORN J. LEGHORN

   "As a youngster I had seen a vaudeville act with this hard-of-hearing sheriff, and this fellow would say, 'Say! P-pay attenshun. I'm ah talkin' to ya, boy.' And I thought that this might make a good character if we made a big Southern rooster out of him. And his voice came out like this: 'I say, pay attenshun, boy. You lookin' for chickens? You see dat little house over there that says D-O-G? Well, that spells chicken. Go get 'em, boy.' "

8. THE TASMANIAN DEVIL

   "When they asked me to do the voice for the Tasmanian Devil, I asked what he sounded like. They said that nobody had ever heard one. So, I created this voice that sounds like a tornado of sound effects. It's another hard one to do."

9. WOODY WOODPECKER

   "When I was in high school, I used to run down this long hallway and I'd do this laugh because I loved the echo. When Walter Lantz asked me to create Woody's trademark laugh, I did my hallway laugh and added a little hacking sound at the end. Then when I contracted with Warner Brothers, I couldn't do Woody anymore, so he had to find somebody else. Turned out to be a woman named Gracie Stafford, who not only did Woody's voice, but also became Mrs. Lantz. Guess Walt didn't want to risk losing another voice."

10. ELMER FUDD
11. ROAD RUNNER
12. HENRY HAWK
13. SPEEDY GONZALES
14. PEPE LE PEW

MEL BLANC'S LIST OF 14 HIGHLY RECOGNIZABLE VOICES OF FILM STARS

Blanc, of course, is not only an expert but a connoisseur of voices. To him, the following are some of the most recognizable voices on the screen today, in alphabetical order.

1. MARLON BRANDO
2. BETTE DAVIS
3. KIRK DOUGLAS
4. HENRY FONDA
5. JANE FONDA
6. KATHARINE HEPBURN
7. PATRICIA NEAL
8. GREGORY PECK
9. VINCENT PRICE
10. JIMMY STEWART
11. BARBRA STREISAND
12. ORSON WELLES
13. JAMES WHITMORE
14. SHELLEY WINTERS

KAY GABLE'S TOP 20 CLARK GABLE MOVIES

Clark Gable's fifth wife and widow, Kay Gable, insists that she is not really a movie buff, even though she and Gable met while she was an actress under contract to MGM in the 1930s. She is, however, a staunch fan of her late husband's films. He was crowned the King of Hollywood in 1938 by columnist Ed Sullivan, and Myrna Loy was crowned Queen. Gable didn't relinquish his title until his untimely death in 1960 from a heart attack. Though the King is gone, his films continue to entertain and delight, and will for generations to come. Here, truly, was a star of all ages.

1. THE MISFITS (1961)
   With Marilyn Monroe, Montgomery Clift. "This was Clark's favorite film, and was well ahead of its time. He worked harder on this than any other of his films, and it may have killed him . . . it was his last movie. It was Marilyn's last movie, too."
2. GONE WITH THE WIND (1939)
   With Vivien Leigh, Leslie Howard, Thomas Mitchell, Olivia de Havilland.

Though one of the most difficult films of his career, *The Misfits* (1961) was Clark Gable's favorite. Marilyn Monroe and Montgomery Clift costarred with him.

"Every frame is a masterpiece. Clark should have gotten the Oscar for it."

3. IT HAPPENED ONE NIGHT (1934)

Gable won the Best Actor Oscar for his role of a reporter hiding a runaway heiress, Claudette Colbert. "This was his most charming movie, it really was."

4. MUTINY ON THE BOUNTY (1935)
   With Charles Laughton, Franchot Tone.
5. SAN FRANCISCO (1936)
   With Spencer Tracy, Jeanette MacDonald
6. BOOM TOWN (1940)
   With Spencer Tracy, Claudette Colbert, Hedy Lamarr
7. TEST PILOT (1938)
   With Spencer Tracy, Myrna Loy
8. IDIOT'S DELIGHT (1939)
   With Norma Shearer
9. TOO HOT TO HANDLE (1938)
   With Myrna Loy
10. HONKY TONK (1941)
    With Lana Turner
11. ADVENTURE (1945)
    With Greer Garson
12. CALL OF THE WILD (1935)
    With Loretta Young
13. THE HUCKSTERS (1947)
    With Deborah Kerr, Ava Gardner
14. MOGAMBO (1953)
    With Grace Kelly, Ava Gardner
15. TEACHER'S PET (1958)
    With Doris Day
16. IT STARTED IN NAPLES (1960)
    With Sophia Loren
17. RUN SILENT, RUN DEEP (1958)
    With Burt Lancaster
18. COMMAND DECISION (1948)
    With Walter Pidgeon
19. HOMECOMING (1948)
    With Lana Turner
20. TO PLEASE A LADY (1950)
    With Barbara Stanwyck

ELEANOR POWELL'S LIST OF 10 UNFORGETTABLE MOMENTS IN HER CAREER

Eleanor Powell came to the screen as "The World's Greatest Tap Dancer," a citation from the New York Dancing Masters of America. When she first attempted to break into Broadway productions in the 1920s, she knew nothing about tap; her particular talents were ballet and acrobatic dancing. When she learned that there was no demand for those things, and that what she needed was tap, she invested thirty-five dollars in ten lessons. It was all she needed. Her natural ability made her famous in New York, and in 1934 Hollywood beckoned. Debuting in a small, but memorable, role in *George White's Scandals* (1935), she was noticed by Louis B. Mayer, who called her to MGM to audition her for the Una Merkel role in *Broadway Melody of 1936*. After seeing her, he realized her potential and created a new role for her as the star of the film. When she said that she didn't know anything about being a star, Mayer told her, "Don't worry about a thing, honey, I'll tell you what to do. You just keep dancing." And she did. She danced her way through thirteen films and into motion picture immortality.

When the Vagabond Theatre in Los Angeles held a retrospective of her films in 1980, the fans lined up around the block. Hating to see them standing in line for several hours to get into the theatre, Powell went outside to visit with them and to sign autographs. She chatted with them for two hours, and at one point even demonstrated a famous step when asked to do so by a young lady who wanted to learn it.

1. "The first joyful meeting with Fred Astaire and our rehearsals together for *Broadway Melody of 1940,* in which we did the 'Begin the Beguine' number." Astaire and she worked together only once because he didn't like working as hard as she did.
2. "The incomparable billing that Arturo Toscanini gave me at our illustrious meeting at MGM in 1935." After Powell danced for him, Toscanini, one of this century's greatest composer-conductors, said: "Now I have seen it all. The Grand Canyon, the glorious California sunset, and your dancing with the noise."
3. "The hours I spent with the great Scottish comedian, Sir Harry Lauder, in Scotland after meeting him while playing the London Palladium in 1949."
4. "The unforgettable meeting with Helen Keller at Radio City Music Hall in 1933, at which time I was doing nine shows a day—five at the Music Hall and four at the New York Center Theatre."
5. "The opening night at the Winter Garden Theatre in 1936 in *At Home Abroad,* while across the street at the Capitol Theatre my first major film, *Broadway Melody of 1936,* was playing; plus my radio show, 'The Flying Red Horse Tavern,' was also on the air. A Broadway show, a film, and a radio program, all going at the same time."
6. "My first job at the Club Martens in Atlantic City at age thirteen in 1925;

Eleanor Powell, "The World's Greatest Tap Dancer," made musical film history with Fred Astaire and George Murphy in MGM's *Broadway Melody of 1940*.

working with Joe Venuti, violin, Eddie Lang, guitar, and Vic Burton, drums. I did acrobatic dancing."

7. "The hilarious hours I spent recording records with Tommy Dorsey at RCA, after filming *Ship Ahoy* with him in 1942." For their biggest hit together,"You Are My Lucky Star,' she is heard tap dancing on a door; it was an improvisation she came up with when she realized that the recording booths all had carpeted floors.

8. "The special friendship and joy of dancing with Bill Robinson, John Bubbles, and others in New York." Robinson taught her his famous "stairs dance," which she performs in *Honolulu* (1939). Robinson taught his dance to only one other—Shirley Temple.

9. "The thrill of receiving five Emmy Awards for teaching Sunday school on my TV show, 'Faith of Our Children' (1954–56). It had nothing to do with dancing."

10. "Thirteen is my lucky number. Thirteen letters in my name; I was thirteen years old in my first theatrical engagement; there are thirteen letters in my home state of Massachusetts; I made thirteen films."

14 CHAPTER

BEYOND THE BLUE HORIZON

Or: *Behind the Scenes and Some Best-Laid Plans*

5 FAMOUS CECIL B. DeMILLE ANECDOTES

Cecil B. DeMille was one of the pioneer filmmakers who put Hollywood on the map, and in the bargain staked out a substantial piece of the area for himself. Almost singlehandedly, he created the movie spectacle, and made Biblical epics, such as *Sign of the Cross* (1931), popular with his liberal use of sex and violence. "But the Bible's pages," he was fond of saying, "are more violence and sex than I could ever portray on the screen."

He was a man of dimensions, strong likes and dislikes, ironclad opinions, and idiosyncratic ways of doing things. DeMille was in all things an original, with many friends, many enemies, many admirers, and many detractors. A man like that, who becomes a legend in his own lifetime, leaves behind not only an impressive sea of work, but countless wonderful stories and anecdotes about that which made him legendary.

1. Perhaps the most famous DeMille story involves a massive scene for one of his spectacles. It could've been *Union Pacific* (1939) or *The Buccaneer* (1938), or another of that era. Because of its incredible complexity, huge cast, and involved special effects, four cameras were set up to record the

scene, which could be done one time only. Preparations were done, and DeMille called, "Action!" Once the smoke cleared, and the scene was over, DeMille turned to his first camera to ask how it looked. The first camera got fouled up with the smoke and didn't get anything. Well, how about the second camera? That big explosion put them out of commission, and they didn't get anything either. What about the third? The camera got knocked over in the action and didn't get a frame of film. DeMille sighed deeply, ready to slash his wrists, when he remebered the fourth camera on the hill which was to record the master shot. Suddenly jubilant, he grabbed the walkie talkie and asked the cameraman on the hill how it looked to him. His reply was: "Ready when you are, C.B."

2. On *The Crusades,* working in a village set with hundreds of extras, DeMille had been pushing everyone very hard to finish a particular sequence. They'd been at it since dawn and it was well into the afternoon without a break. One of the things that DeMille would not tolerate on his set was talking when they were trying to set up a shot. Suddenly his attention was drawn to a dress extra who was talking with her girlfriend. In a rage, DeMille stormed to her, practically parting the Red Sea in his fury. "What do you mean by talking after I have called for silence?" he demanded. All eyes and ears were on DeMille and the extra who blushed hotly. "Since what you had to say was that important, I want you to repeat it so everyone on the set can hear you!" he commanded. After a quick breath of resignation, she said, "If you really want to know, I asked my friend when that bald-headed old sonuvabitch was going to call lunch." You could have knocked him over with a feather. The stunned silence was broken by DeMille's thundering, *"Lunch!"*

3. It was an obsession with DeMille to have quiet on the set. "I don't want to have to shout," he used to say, "a simple instruction to somebody only a few feet away. If it's quiet, I don't have to." If it wasn't quiet, he'd banish the violator. Once he banished his own daughter, Agnes, for talking during a rehearsal. Another time it was Hedda Hopper. And when he was directing, he almost never left the set. So, you can imagine the surprise of his secretary when he turned up in the office in the middle of the day, during the production of a picture. "What happened, Mr. DeMille?" she asked. "Did you talk on the set?"

4. DeMille loved his work, and was very proud of his films. He took great delight and satisfaction in the many awards he won. On the night he was honored with the Milestone Award by the Screen Producers' Guild, he was asked how many Oscars he'd won. "Eleven," he answered, then added: "But they only gave me three."

5. One of DeMille's favorite tools was the "Jody version." In the early stages of a story's development, he'd say, "All right, let's do a Jody version." Jody was his seven-year-old grandson at the time the system was inaugurated; seems C.B. was having trouble with a current story. It was getting

enes like this with Elissa Landi in *Sign of the Cross* (1932) made DeMille's
plical epics big box office and brought him much criticism from the clergy, who
id he infused too much sex and violence into the Bible.

too messy and complicated, so he asked for two pages of what it was about. These he took home and read to Jody. If Jody started to squirm, it was not good. Often, Jody was able to pinpoint something in the story that didn't work. DeMille is said to have used this technique long after Jody had grown up.

CHARLTON HESTON'S LIST OF 8 CHARACTERISTIC ATTITUDES OF CECIL B. DeMILLE TOWARD ACTORS

Charlton Heston was first introduced to Cecil B. DeMille when he came out to Hollywood from New York to work for Hal Wallis in a forgettable picture called *Dark City* (1950). Two years later he became a star in DeMille's *The Greatest Show on Earth;* it was his second film. He again worked for the legendary director/producer in *The Ten Commandments* (1956), in which Heston portrayed Moses, in the career-making role of his life. He has since then been the actor most identified with epic motion pictures.

Heston: 'I'm not certain that my early film beginnings with DeMille influenced my career into the epic genre. It's·certainly a persuasive idea, but not necessarily true, because my whole experience was rooted in this area. I was trained on the stage in Shakespeare. My first part on Broadway was in Shakespeare, which is of course epic theatre. I guess I simply am more castable than others in this genre, a point that DeMille helped establish. Certainly the two films I did for him made me a marketable, bankable commodity, which is what a star career requires. But," he adds ironically, "it also created a pigeonhole from which I make unrelenting and vigorous attempts to escape.

"He always treated me marvelously, and, as far as I know, always spoke of me generously. At the same time, he had a reputation of being an ogre. I dare say it was well earned. I knew him only in his last years when he'd mellowed somewhat, but I'm told he used to be quite a Tartar. But he was seldom hard on actors."

The following list is characteristic, in Heston's experience, of just exactly how DeMille treated and regarded actors:

1. "From the point of view of the Screen Actors Guild, DeMille's preoccupation with Hollywood as a production center was valuable indeed. With the obvious exceptions of his use of necessary locations, he shot nearly every foot of his films in Hollywood. This is quite unique today, and was even in his later years. He hired a lot of actors and he hired them here. And he would keep them employed for long periods of time.

Charlton Heston, with James Stewart (the clown) and Cornel Wilde, in *The Greatest Show on Earth* (1952), his first of two films for Cecil B. DeMille.

2. "He liked performers, not extras. To that end, he did something that is rare today, and was indeed rare in his day. He would employ what amounted to a stock company of about a dozen utility players. These were actors with no specific roles, but he carried them through the picture

at scale, so that if he wanted to give somebody a line in a scene, he didn't have to give it to an extra.

3. "It was also common knowledge among the older actors and bit players in Hollywood that if DeMille were shooting a picture between November and January, there would be a big scene scheduled with a lot of small parts which would be carried for two or three weeks just before Christmas. This goes back to a freer, easier time when production costs weren't so prohibitive, but it was, nonetheless, his practice. This was not unique to him; John Ford did the same thing. But it was absolutely typical of DeMille.

4. "His casting interviews were unique in my experience. As far as I know, it was a routine he invariably followed. If he was considering you for a part, he'd ask you to come in. He had a huge, cluttered, and quite fascinating office, about twenty-five feet across, jammed with memorabilia, models and awards, paintings and props, and all sorts of odds and ends from his films. He would sit at his desk or walk about the room, pointing out story boards or development sketches or set models or costume designs while telling you the story of the picture from the point of view of your character. But he'd never say, 'I'm considering you for this part.' He would never show you a script, and certainly would never have you *read* for a part. He'd merely talk about it, which left you at a loss for a response. You couldn't say, 'Well, I think I could do that,' because the question had never come up. Through the half-dozen interviews for the circus picture, and roughly the same number for Moses, all I could say was, 'Certainly is interesting. Sounds like it will make a fine film.' What else could you say? The touchy subject of your capabilities for the role never came up.

5. "He was usually remarkably, even elaborately, courteous to actors. He almost always addressed a company as 'Ladies and gentlemen.' Even with extras, his personal manner was punctiliously courteous. I found his formality and old-fashioned manners very attractive.

6. "His rages on the set, during which he'd chew out assistants and technicians, were legendary. I think he used these theatrical rages to make an impression on the actors without disturbing them directly. For example, if an actress were consistently late to the set each morning, he would not chew her out. He would instead chew out her hairdresser, ruthlessly, to the verge of tears. Obviously, this would have some effect on the actress.

7. "Only a few times did I see him rip up an actor; and this happened only when he thought the actor was loafing, or oddly enough (and perhaps unfairly) if he thought the actor was a physical coward. Not that he expected actors to do everything they were pretending to do in the film, of course. But he himself was a very brave man, and if he decided that an actor was afraid to do things that DeMille knew were within his capabilities, the Old Man would cloud up and fall down on him.

8. "I also saw him more patient with an actor than I have ever seen a director; much more patient than I would have been. There was a bit player, a member of the stock company that I mentioned above, on the circus picture, who I saw blow more takes than I've ever seen an actor blow. He muffed twenty-seven straight takes. It has to be a record. (Maybe there's a list there.) I'll never forget the line: 'Hey, Brad, Holly's spinnin' like a weather vane in a Kansas twister.' But somehow, the actor just could not get that line out. Finally, after two hours of takes, DeMille had to replace him. And during that time, he never spoke sharply to the man; he was infinitely patient. That was the other side of the 'monster.'"

20 FAMOUS FILMS AND THEIR ORIGINAL CASTING NOTIONS

Odd as it may seem, it is indeed rare for a film to actually make it to the screen with the stars who are the first choices for the major roles; and sometimes even with the actors who are first contracted to do the picture. Had the original casting notions actually been effected, many of the classic motion pictures as we know them today would have been vastly different—or would not have become classics at all.

1. FRANKENSTEIN (1931)
   The first actor to be considered for the part of the monster was Bela Lugosi, who was a sensation in *Dracula* earlier that year. But he wanted no part of it (though he got around to playing the role in 1943 in *Frankenstein Meets the Wolf Man*). Then came John Carradine, also under contract to Universal at the time, who was told to report to makeup to get made up as the monster for testing. He said that he hadn't studied acting for so long and so hard to play monsters, and refused. The part then fell to Boris Karloff. It made him a star. And in retrospect it's hard to imagine anyone else in that original screen interpretation.

2. TARZAN THE APE MAN (1932)
   Can you picture this film with Herman Brix, instead of Johnny Weissmuller? Yet Brix, an Olympic shotput champ who later changed his name to Bruce Bennett, was the first choice. But when he was injured in his first film, *Touchdown,* the part went to Weissmuller, who became, for several generations, *the* Tarzan of the movies. Brix subsequently played the role in a 1935 serial, *The New Adventures of Tarzan,* hand-picked by Tarzan's creator, Edgar Rice Burroughs, who also produced the chapter play.

3. THE WIZARD OF OZ (1939)
   Producer Mervyn Le Roy did everything in his power to get 20th Century-Fox star Shirley Temple for the role of Dorothy, but Darryl F. Zan-

uck wouldn't go along. So MGM contract player Judy Garland inherited the part. W. C. Fields had been intended for the role of the Wizard, but money negotiations bogged down and Frank Morgan literally begged for the part and got it. Buddy Ebsen was signed to play the Tinman, but in early makeup tests, he contracted a lung infection from the metallic body paint and was unable to do it; he was replaced by Jack Haley. And Margaret Hamilton, that immortal Wicked Witch of the West, won the part only after Le Roy decided that front-runner Gale Sondergaard was too glamourous. What kind of picture would this beloved classic have been with: Shirley Temple, W. C. Fields, Buddy Ebsen, and Gale Sondergaard? Very different.

4. GONE WITH THE WIND (1939)

There was more publicity about the casting for Margaret Mitchell's sweeping novel of the Civil War than for any other film in the history of Hollywood. Producer David O. Selznick, who made casting an art, kept the world in suspense as he tried to fill the major roles to everyone's satisfaction. His first choice for Rhett Butler was none other than Gary Cooper. But he couldn't get him. There was some talk about Errol Flynn. Though the role went to Clark Gable, it hadn't been confirmed yet when the role of Scarlett O'Hara was offered to Bette Davis, who refused because she didn't want to risk having to do the film with Flynn, whom she despised. The fact that Selznick eventually discovered Vivien Leigh only days before production was to commence was one of the best-kept publicity secrets of the day.

5. THE MALTESE FALCON (1941)

No one but Humphrey Bogart could have played Sam Spade, right? Yet, first choice was George Raft, who turned it down because he didn't want to work with the new director in town, John Huston. He had earlier turned down *Dead End* (1937) which then went to Bogart; and later rejected *High Sierra* (1941) which also fell to Bogart. In retrospect, perhaps Raft had as much to do with Bogey's success as anybody.

6. CASABLANCA (1943)

Warner Brothers contract player Ronald Reagan, who'd scored big in *King's Row* (1941), was lined up to co-star with Ann Sheridan in a medium budget film called *Everybody Goes to Rick's*. But in trying to capitalize on Humphrey Bogart's rocketing popularity, the project was given to him, with a bigger budget, a new leading lady, Ingrid Bergman, and a new title, *Casablanca*.

7. SUNSET BOULEVARD (1950)

Though her performance in this film was the best of her career, Gloria Swanson got the part only after director Billy Wilder was unable to talk Mae West into it. And William Holden's part of a lifetime would have been Montgomery Clift's but for the fact that Clift found the role distasteful in its parallels between his real-life friendship with the notorious

Gloria Swanson and William Holden gave unforgettable performances in *Sunset Boulevard* (1950), but were cast only after Mae West and Montgomery Clift had turned down the parts.

Most of the major roles in *From Here to Eternity* (1953) ended up being recast before the film went into production. Ernest Borgnine, Frank Sinatra, and Montgomery Clift were all second choices for their parts.

Libby Holman and the script's central relationship between the young opportunistic writer and the aging movie queen.

8. FROM HERE TO ETERNITY (1953)

There has been much speculation about the cast-shuffling of this particular film; some of which was allegedly the basis of part of the plot in Mario Puzo's best-selling novel, *The Godfather*. For example, Eli Wallach had been set by Columbia boss Harry Cohn to play the plum role of Maggio, but Wallach mysteriously withdrew and Frank Sinatra got the part, which won him an Oscar and gave him a new career. Aldo Ray was supposed to play the Monty Clift role, but director Fred Zinneman refused to do the picture unless Clift had the part. Cohn conceded again. Except for the fact that both Joan Crawford and Rita Hayworth rejected the part, it might not have been Deborah Kerr rolling around in the surf in that very famous love scene with Burt Lancaster. Kerr rolled her way into a well-deserved Oscar nomination—thanks to Hayworth and Crawford.

9. A STAR IS BORN (1954)

Unwilling to deal with Judy Garland's tantrums and scene-stealing, Marlon Brando, Cary Grant, Henry Fonda, and Errol Flynn all turned down the sensational part that won James Mason an Academy Award nomination.

10. BEN-HUR (1959)

    William Wyler had Burt Lancaster all lined up for the title role, but he backed out, deciding that he would look silly in Biblical costume. Charlton Heston, who took the part, has made a career in Biblical wardrobe. Cecil B. DeMille once said of Heston: "He has a face that looks at home in an era."

11. VERTIGO (1958)

    While under personal contract to Alfred Hitchcock, Vera Miles was set to costar with Jimmy Stewart in *Vertigo*, which was developed and written expressly for her. She was in the early stage of pregnancy with her third child, Michael, when the picture was scheduled to start. However, various things delayed production so that by the time Hitch was ready to roll, Vera had begun to show, and could no longer do the part. Having to face the bad news, Hitch told her: "Don't you know it's bad taste to have more than two?" Bad taste or not, her baby was much more important than a movie, and Hitch begrudgingly replaced her with look-alike, Kim Novak.

12. LAWRENCE OF ARABIA (1962)

    Marlon Brando was the first choice for *Lawrence*. How lucky for Peter O'Toole, and the rest of us, that Brando's excesses on *Mutiny on the Bounty* kept him in Tahiti for months longer than scheduled, and he was unable to do the role. Director David Lean then cast relatively unknown O'Toole, who became a star and earned an Academy Award nomination. Lean later said, without naming any names, "When you create a star, you create a monster."

13. MY FAIR LADY (1964)

    It greatly amused Cary Grant when Warner Brothers chief, Jack Warner, offered him the part of Henry Higgins. Grant said that a cockney was hardly the person to be teaching elocution to the pygmalion, Eliza Doolittle and insisted instead that pal Rex Harrison be given the chance to re-create his smash Broadway performance. Warner nodded, and then offered the part to James Cagney, who didn't spark to it. So Harrison ended up with it, doing such a great job that it's difficult to conjure up anyone who could have matched him.

14. THE GRADUATE (1967)

    Picture this if you can: Robert Redford cavorting in the sack with Mrs. Robinson. Can't, huh? Well, director Mike Nichols could, because he tried to get the then-thirty-one-year-old Redford to do the film, but Redford felt that he couldn't bring the proper amount of youthful naïveté to the role. So, the part went to the then-thirty-year-old Dustin Hoffman, who catapulted to overnight stardom in one of the most popular films of all time, winning his first Oscar nomination in his debut film. Anne

Bancroft's Oscar-nomination role of Mrs. Robinson almost went to Susan Hayward, who rejected it because she found the role distasteful, and to Doris Day, who also found it too contrary to her nice-as-pie image.

15. BONNIE AND CLYDE (1967)
When Tuesday Weld was unable to costar opposite Warren Beatty, the role of Bonnie Parker went to Faye Dunaway. It proved to be a fortuitous fill-in for Dunaway, as the film became not only a cinema technique trend setter, but a career-making vehicle, winning Academy Award nominations for Beatty, Dunaway, Gene Hackman, and Estelle Parsons. Also for the film and director Arthur Penn.

16. BUTCH CASSIDY AND THE SUNDANCE KID (1969)
Almost from the first page of the script, the two engaging lead roles were fashioned for Paul Newman and Steve McQueen. Reasons as to why McQueen didn't do the film are a bit muddled. Was it billing, or money, or conflicting commitments? Whatever the reason, it was indeed a break for Robert Redford, whose career had been languishing. This film, partially because of Newman's expert underplaying, revealed him as a powerful, charismatic star.

17. MIDNIGHT COWBOY (1969)
This first X-rated film to win an Oscar as Best Picture was originally intended for Michael Sarrazin in the Jon Voight role. Voight's performance opposite Dustin Hoffman was brilliant; both won Oscar nominations as Best Actor, but lost to John Wayne for *True Grit*. Voight didn't care; he got the star-making part.

18. KING KONG (1976)
Producer Dino De Laurentiis badly wanted Bo Derek for the apple of King Kong's eye, but despite the potential of its being a blockbuster, John Derek felt it wasn't the right vehicle for her and they declined. Time has proven them right. Jessica Lange, who took the Fay Wray retread, hasn't found it to have been a particularly star-building role. As for Bo Derek, her film debut was made in *Orca* (1977), a forgettable big fish story from De Laurentiis. It was her only filmwork until she scored high in *10*.

19. A STAR IS BORN (1976)
Barbra Streisand personally pitched Elvis Presley to costar with her in her·remake of *A Star is Born*. She met with him between shows in his Caesar's Palace dressing room to outline her ideas for the film. There was an initial wave of enthusiasm, but Presley ultimately rejected playing a has-been rock star, and, the story goes, he didn't want to be bossed around by La Streisand on a film set where she called all the shots. Kris Kristofferson ended up with the film role. Who knows what it could have done for Presley's film career? Without doubt it would have been the first Class A picture to his credit.

20. 10 (1979)

It's hard to say anything about this picture that hasn't already seen print elsewhere. Of course, it was the picture to catapult Bo Derek, then an unknown, into international stardom as the first sex symbol of the 1980s. It also made a newly castable star of Dudley Moore, who was recruited at the midnight hour by director Blake Edwards to replace the departed star, George Segal, who quit after production started because of "creative differences." That usually means somebody else is getting all the good lines, or all the close-ups. And in 10, who was deserving of a really good close-up, other than you-know-who?

STAN CORWIN'S LIST OF 9 BEST-SELLERS THAT WERE SOLD TO THE MOVIES, BUT NEVER MADE IT TO THE SCREEN

Stanley J. Corwin is president of Stan Corwin Productions, Ltd., producing films and books in association with major film companies and book publishers; and is also president of the Los Angeles media company, Dana/Corwin Enterprises. As the former president and publisher of Pinnacle Books, the first major New York book publisher to relocate to the West Coast, Corwin has not only given new meaning to the term "bi-coastalism," but he has had a hand in the creation of more than one best-seller.

States Corwin: "Here are some sensational book properties that were snapped up by Hollywood producers, at some very hefty prices, but for some reason or other never quite made it into production":

1. FEAR OF FLYING

"The outrageous best-seller of the seventies by Erica Jong, which had nothing to do with airplanes. What a great movie it would make, but it hasn't."

2. FOOLS DIE

"The Mario Puzo sequel, after they make *Godfather III* through *XVII.*"

3. FIRE ISLAND

"The torrid explosive novel still yearning to steam up the screen. Once they figure out what to do with it . . ."

4. THE GEMINI CONTENDERS

"Great Ludlum, but too difficult and expensive to film—or so they've been saying."

5. THE THORN BIRDS

"*The* best-seller of the late seventies that romanced its way to the top of the charts for some nine months and almost gave birth to a Robert Redford-starring *Gone With the Wind*, Aussie-style—but didn't."

6. TAIPAN
Early James Clavell, before *Shōgun,* which had been on the boards for years as a Steve McQueen starrer. Now, it will surely get filmed.

7. MAN'S FATE
"Andre Malraux's masterwork has collected lots of option money, and someday may even become a major film."

8. THE LOVE MACHINE
"A Jacqueline Susann 'Valley of the Delicious,' with meaty roles for everybody.

9. THE FAN CLUB
"Irving Wallace's sexy sizzler waiting to be turned into a film fantasy."

HARVEY PERRY'S LIST OF 7 MOVIE STUNT TRAGEDIES

One of the deans of motion picture stuntmen, Harvey Perry, at eighty in 1980, is still doing pratfalls and film stunts. A natural athlete with national championship titles in boxing and diving, Perry began in filmwork in 1919. Originally, because of his small size (5'7") he doubled for women, but through the years he has doubled practically every big star in Hollywood history including Tom Mix, Kirk Douglas, Errol Flynn, Alan Ladd, Burt Lancaster, Bob Mitchum, Tony Curtis, even John Wayne.

Remarks Perry: "Wayne was so damn big that the only way I could get away with doubling him was in a long shot. It was on *The Big Trail* in 1930 for Raoul Walsh. I did some riding in a real long shot. Mostly, I doubled for all the midgets over at Warners like Bogart, Cagney, Raft, Robinson, and the like.

"It's hard to train anybody to be a stuntman. The best ones have all been professional athletes or acrobats. In this business, you're only as good as your last pratfall . . . and because it is a dangerous occupation, you're constantly injuring yourself. And sometimes, a guy gets killed, too."

1. TRAIL OF '98 (1928)
"MGM sent a second unit up to Cordova, Alaska, to shoot the Copper River Rapids. It was freezing cold; the river plummeted through the rocks and ice at twenty-two miles per hour into a huge gorge which was eighteen feet deep in places, then down into a glacial lake. Even with safety precautions, four stuntmen lost their lives in that river: One was buried in the gorge by an avalanche of ice and snow; of four men who were carried away by the rushing water, only one was found, badly battered

against the rocks. The terrible irony of it was that when the footage was viewed back at the studio, it was decided that it looked unrealistic, like a miniature, and wasn't even used.''

2. THE CHARGE OF THE LIGHT BRIGADE (1936)
   "The climax of the picture was this thundering charge into certain death by the British army. I remember the director, Michael Curtiz, telling everybody not to draw your sabre during the charge. There was this one guy named Fred Butterworth who thought it would look good in the shot, and drew his sword. He fell from his horse onto the sword which went through him to the hilt. There was irony here, too, personal irony. Butterworth had just inherited a large amount of money and was going to retire.''

3. TARZAN AND THE MERMAIDS (1948)
   "Stuntman Angel Garcia was killed on location when, completing a spectacular dive from the high Acapulco Cliffs, a wave unexpectedly smashed him against the rocks.''

4. THE HORSE SOLDIERS (1959)
   "Fred Kennedy was killed doing a saddle fall for William Holden. The horse fell on him.''

Errol Flynn rides at the head of the British regiment in *Charge of the Light Brigade* (1936), during the filming of which a stuntman fell onto his sword and was killed.

5. HOW THE WEST WAS WON (1963)

"Veteran stuntman Bob Morgan lost a leg, an eye, and had a bowel torn out in an accident. It was pretty damn awful. I don't know how he survived, but he did. You wouldn't have given a plugged nickel for his chances right after, but he made it. Being in top physical shape pulled him through."

6. THE HALLELUJAH TRAIL (1965)

"I never could figure this one out. It never should've happened. Bill Williams was killed driving a covered wagon off a mountain ridge. He should have jumped clear but he didn't. Or couldn't. We'll never know what happened."

7. THE FLIGHT OF THE PHOENIX (1966)

"Paul Mantz, who was one helluva good flyer, was diving toward the ground and lost his motor. Somehow he pulled her up and kept her from crashing, but the wheels caught in the sand and the plane went end on end. It killed Mantz and crippled Bobby Rose pretty good. Rose had been one of the survivors of that terrible *Trail of '98* tragedy."

Comments Prry: "There have been lots of accidents and deaths in this business, and I don't like to talk about it much. This is just a handful of stuff that's happened. Sometimes I wonder if it's really worth it. I guess we must think it is, 'cause we go right on making pictures and taking chances."

HARVEY PERRY'S LIST OF 8 OF THE BEST STUNTMEN EVER

Says Perry: "You know what this is: it's a crap shoot. Everybody has their favorites, guys you like the best, maybe because they can do a stunt better'n you, or maybe because they've got more style. It'll be hard to get two stuntmen to agree to the same names to go on a list like this. So, if I were making the list, I'd have to say the top two are Davie Sharp and Richard Talmadge, or the other way around, and the others will have to be in special order, except that I don't know if you could leave them off and have the list be worth a damn."

1. RICHARD TALMADGE

"He started doubling for Douglas Fairbanks. He was better-looking than most of us stuntmen, so he started to get acting parts, and became a silent movie star. Then when talkies came in, he lost his new career because of a lousy, high speaking voice. He went right back to stunts. He was probably the best all-around stuntman ever. And that's saying one helluva lot."

2. DAVE SHARPE

"Dave was the kind of guy who could do a twenty-five-foot fall off a building onto concrete without any kind of padding. He was that good. He could take a small stunt and make it great. Being a champion gymnast was what did it. Gave him control over his body like you couldn't believe; he was completely coordinated. Along with Talmadge, he stands legendary in this business."

3. YAKIMA CANUTT

"He was one of your all-time great Western action men."

4. JOE YRIOGOYEN

"Probably the best horseman who ever lived."

5. RED MORGAN

"How can you leave him off a list like this?"

6. HAL NEEDHAM

"I've never particularly been a fan of his, but he was as good a daredevil stuntman as you can get. He would do with sheer nerve what Dave Sharpe would do with ability."

7. JOCK MAHONEY

"For a big guy, he was about as gifted as you can get. There was very little he couldn't do. What a jumper!"

8. DAR ROBINSON

"Of the new breed, who can figure things out like a science, he's the best."

 **THE GROOVE TUBE**

Or: *How Movies and TV Became Reluctant Bedfellows*

CHAPTER

10 REVEALING HOLLYWOOD QUOTES ABOUT THE ADVENT OF TELEVISION

1. LOUIS B. MAYER, MGM studio executive
   "It's a plague and a curse, and I won't have any of our people working on it. And we certainly won't sell them any of our motion pictures."
2. SAM GOLDWYN, producer
   "Why should people go out and pay money to see bad movies, when they can see bad television at home for nothing?"
3. BILLY WILDER, producer/director
   "I'm delighted with it because it used to be that films were the lowest form of art. Now we have something to look down on."
4. CECIL B. DeMILLE, producer/director
   "You're not going to wipe out theatres with home television or anything else. You just have to give the audience a good reason to go out to the theatre, that's all."
5. DARRYL F. ZANUCK, 20th Century-Fox studio chief
   "Video won't be able to hold onto any market it captures after the first six months. People will soon get tired of staring at a plywood box every night."
6. JOHN WAYNE
   "Sure, I was offered a series, but I turned it down. It's not that I look

down my nose at television, but you have to admit movies are more important."
7. BOB HOPE
"The big pictures this year have had some intriguing themes—sex, perversion, adultery, and cannibalism. They'll get those kids away from their TV sets yet."
8. BING CROSBY
"Well, I'd say it's pretty good, considering it's for nothing."
9. FRANK CAPRA, director
"Working in television is the same as working in movies. TV is simply a private theatre in every home as far as I'm concerned."
10. HARRY COHN, Columbia Studio Chief
" . . . and you tell the prop boys that I better not see an idiot box in any of the interior sets."

12 WELL-KNOWN MOVIE ACTORS WHOSE PRESENCE IN A TV PILOT WASN'T QUITE ENOUGH TO SELL IT AS A SERIES

In the early days of television, most Hollywood actors shunned TV because it was considered a competitive medium. In fact, many actors' contracts expressly forbade them to perform on television. But as time went on, and the movies went into a depression, many film stars made the crossover. Many thought that all they had to do was to appear, and they would be a success in TV, because, after all, they were already successful in movies. And TV was only an ugly stepchild of the film industry. However, many established movie actors found that their mere presence wasn't quite enough to sell a series. TV success was a little harder to attain than it was at first thought.

1. ANN SHERIDAN, "Calling Terry Conway" (1956)
2. CELESTE HOLM, "Carolyn" (1956); "Meet Me in St. Louis" (1966)
3. MAMIE VAN DOREN, "Meet the Girls" (1960)
4. MARGARET O'BRIEN, "Maggie" (1960)
5. JOHN PAYNE, "O'Connor's Ocean" (1960)
6. CLAUDETTE COLBERT, "Welcome to Washington" (1960)
7. GINGER ROGERS, "A Love Affair Just for Three" (1963)
8. ETHEL MERMAN, "Maggie Brown" (1963)
9. BASIL RATHBONE, "Pirates of Flounders Bay" (1966)
10. GILBERT ROLAND, "Land's End" (1968)
11. GLORIA DE HAVEN, "Wednesday Night Out" (1972)
12. VAN JOHNSON, "Wheeler and Murdock" (1972)

A BAKER'S DOZEN MOST-OFTEN-BROADCAST MOVIES ON TV

Movies have always been a staple of television programing, especially on the local level, where original programing is prohibitive. Just which pictures turn up most often in afternoon- and late-show reruns is determined by viewer request, ratings, and the *TV Feature Film Source Book*, which rates nearly every sound motion picture in terms of its appeal to TV audiences. Sometimes a movie's performance in theatres has no direct or automatic relationship to its TV performance. A *TV Guide* poll of programing directors around the country revealed the following as the most-often-played, most-often-requested vintage movies on television:

1. CASABLANCA (1943)
   Humphrey Bogart, Ingrid Bergman, Claude Rains
2. KING KONG (1933)
   Bruce Cabot, Fay Wray, Robert Armstrong

King Kong (1933), the classic beauty-and-beast tale with Fay Wray, has been shown on television more than any other film with the exception of *Casablanca* (1943).

3. THE MAGNIFICENT SEVEN (1960)
   Yul Brynner, Steve McQueen, Charles Bronson, James Coburn, Eli Wallach
4. THE MALTESE FALCON (1941)
   Humphrey Bogart, Mary Astor, Peter Lorre, Sydney Greenstreet
5. THE ADVENTURES OF ROBIN HOOD (1938)
   Errol Flynn, Olivia de Havilland, Basil Rathbone, Claude Rains
6. THE AFRICAN QUEEN (1951)
   Humphrey Bogart, Katharine Hepburn
7. CITIZEN KANE (1941)
   Orson Welles, Joseph Cotten, Agnes Moorehead
8. MIRACLE ON 34TH STREET (1947)
   Maureen O'Hara, Edmund Gwenn, Natalie Wood
9. GIRLS! GIRLS! GIRLS! (1962)
   Elvis Presley, Stella Stevens
10. THE BIRDS (1963)
    Rod Taylor, Tippi Hedren
11. KING SOLOMON'S MINES (1950)
    Stewart Granger, Deborah Kerr
12. TREASURE OF THE SIERRA MADRE (1948)
    Humphrey Bogart, Walter Huston, Tim Holt, Bruce Bennett
13. WAR OF THE WORLDS (1953)
    Gene Barry, Ann Robinson

THE 20 HIGHEST-RATED MOVIES ON TELEVISION

MOVIE	RATING
1. GONE WITH THE WIND (1939)	47.6
Director: Victor Fleming; Clark Gable, Vivien Leigh	
2. AIRPORT (1970)	42.3
D: George Seaton; Burt Lancaster, George Kennedy	
2. LOVE STORY (1970)*	42.3
D: Arthur Hiller; Ali MacGraw, Ryan O'Neal	
4. THE GODFATHER: PART II (1974)	39.4
D: Francis Ford Coppola; Al Pacino, Robert De Niro	
5. JAWS (1975)	39.1
D: Steven Spielberg; Roy Scheider, Richard Dreyfuss	
6. POSEIDON ADVENTURE (1972)	39.0
D: Ronald Neame; Gene Hackman, Ernest Borgnine	
7. TRUE GRIT (1969)	38.9
D: Henry Hathaway; John Wayne, Kim Darby	
7. THE BIRDS (1963)*	38.9
D: Alfred Hitchcock; Rod Taylor, Tippi Hedren	

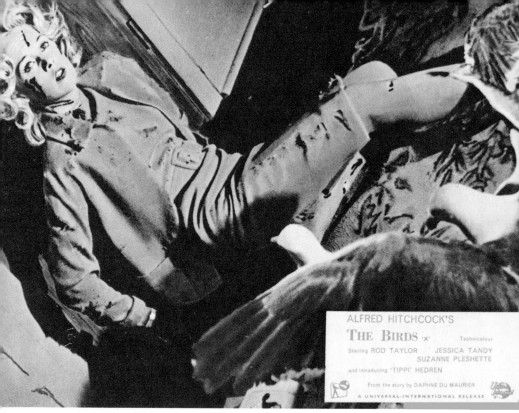

Tippi Hedren recoils in terror as *The Birds* (1963) advance on her.

19. THE SOUND OF MUSIC (1965)   33.6
    D: Robert Wise; Julie Andrews, Christopher Plummer
20. BONNIE AND CLYDE (1967)   33.4
    D: Arthur Penn; Warren Beatty, Faye Dunaway

* Indicates a tie with the film immediately preceding it; hence no numerical change, though it does count toward the total tally.

LOU FERRIGNO'S FAVORITE 4 MUSCLEMAN MOVIES

Even TV's "Incredible Hulk" loves going to the movies. Says the 6'5", 260-lb., hugely developed Ferrigno: "I prefer the classic pictures over the newer things. The plots were a lot better. They were just made better . . . and I grew up on them."

Lou Ferrigno, TV's "The Incredible Hulk," without makeup, would enjoy starring in a remake of *Samson and Delilah*.

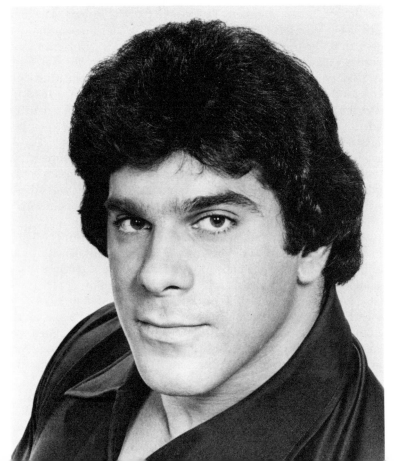

1. *HERCULES* (1959), with Steve Reeves.
2. *HERCULES UNCHAINED* (1960), with Steve Reeves.
3. *SAMSON AND DELILAH* (1949), with Victor Mature.
4. *TARZAN, THE APEMAN* (1932), with Johnny Weissmuller.

"I don't care how many Tarzan movies they make, there will never be another Tarzan like Weissmuller. I wouldn't mind playing Tarzan myself, but I'd rather do a remake of *Hercules* or *Samson and Delilah.*"

4 MOVIES TO WHICH NEW FOOTAGE WAS ADDED FOR TV

Usually, when a motion picture premieres on television, it is considerably shorter than in its theatrical release, having been edited for TV standards and for fitting into a certain time frame. It is rare indeed for the TV version to be longer, or to have new footage. But it does happen. Witness the following:

1. SECRET CEREMONY (1968)
   Director: Joseph Losey; Elizabeth Taylor, Mia Farrow, Robert Mitchum. So much was objectionable about this movie that after the censors got through with it, there was hardly enough to telecast. So, Universal shot extra scenes with a psychiatrist, a sort of wraparound host, like Rod Serling on "Night Gallery," to introduce the picture and explain what was going on, and what happened in the edited sequences. They tried to make the film more acceptable for TV, but they only succeeded in making it stupid.
2. EARTHQUAKE (1974)
   D: Mark Robson; Charlton Heston, Ava Gardner, George Kennedy. A much maligned film which was considerably better than it was given credit for. Additional footage of scenes left on the cutting room floor was added for the first network telecast, giving it more scope and entertainment value.
3. AIRPORT '77 (1977)
   D: Jerry Jameson; Jack Lemmon, Lee Grant, George Kennedy. This third entry in the *Airport* disaster series was one of the better installments, and merited the additional footage added for its TV premiere showing to give it more importance . . . and to fill up a three-hour time slot.
4. THE GODFATHER (1972) and THE GODFATHER PART II (1974)
   D: Francis Ford Coppola; Marlon Brando, James Caan, Al Pacino. In one of the finest programs ever assembled for TV, Coppola edited the two films together and patched holes with unused and heretofore-unseen footage. The result was a nine-hour event: "The Godfather Saga: The

Complete Novel for Television." A masterpiece. One of those rare instances where the whole is even better than its parts.

... AND 1 MOVIE WITH NEW FOOTAGE ADDED FOR ITS THEATRICAL RE-RELEASE

1. CLOSE ENCOUNTERS OF THE THIRD KIND: THE SPECIAL EDITION (1980)
   Director: Steven Spielberg; Richard Dreyfuss, Teri Garr. In a much ballyhooed reissue, the 1977 *Close Encounters* was touted as being a "Special Edition," for which director Spielberg, fresh from *1941* (1979), his Kamikaze version of picture-making, donned his surgical gloves, took out old scenes, added new ones, and created a new experience. As it turned out, the experience wasn't so new—it was one quite familiar to movie audiences: disappointment. Several ticket buyers were so moved by their disappointment that they filed a class action suit against Columbia Studios for false advertising.

3 POPULAR TV SERIES TO INSPIRE THEATRICAL FEATURES

From the advent of the tube in the late 1940s, it was standard procedure to create TV series based on hit motion pictures; several hundred series have been spawned over the years, including such current shows as "The Dukes of Hazzard," which was based on *The Moonrunners* (1974), and "The Valley of the Dolls."

The reverse, where a series inspires a motion picture, is a rarity. But no stone is left unturned by creative producers in search of that elusive buck.

1. OUR MISS BROOKS (1956)
   Director: Al Lewis; Eve Arden, Gale Gordon, Don Porter, Richard Crenna. This situation comedy about a high school teacher began on the radio in 1948 with Eve Arden in the title role; it inspired a TV series (1952–56), which then spawned a feature version with most of the cast intact.
2. THE LONE RANGER (1956)
   D: Stuart Heisler; Clayton Moore, Jay Silverheels, Lyle Bettger. This popular Western began on radio in 1933, and was adapted to several movie serials before embarking on a TV series (1949–57). Its immense popularity inspired an all-new feature version while the series was still in production; and that movie's box-office success led to a second movie with Clayton Moore, *Lone Ranger and the City of Gold* (1958).

3. STAR TREK, THE MOVIE (1979)

D: Robert Wise; William Shatner, Leonard Nimoy, DeForrest Kelly. This TV space odyssey has the largest cult following of any TV series ever. Though only on the air for three seasons (1966–69), "Star Trek"'s devotees (called Trekkies) grew to legion numbers when the series went into syndication, eventually prompting the theatrical reprise. After all the waiting, and millions of dollars spent on the production, *Star Trek, The Movie* was quickly nicknamed *Star Drek*. The series was better.

. . . AND 8 FEATURE FILMS COMPOSED OF SEVERAL TV SERIES EPISODES EDITED TOGETHER AND RELEASED TO THEATRES

1. DAVY CROCKETT, KING OF THE WILD FRONTIER (1955)

Director: Norman Foster; Fess Parker, Buddy Ebsen. Originally filmed and telecast as three one-hour episodes of "Disney's Wonderful World of Color," this phenomenally successful series kicked off the first TV-inspired national craze: coonskin caps and all. And Disney, not being one to miss a bet, quickly edited the shows together and released them theatrically. It couldn't miss. It made a pile of money.

2. DAVY CROCKETT AND THE RIVER PIRATES (1956)

D: Norman Foster; Fess Parker, Buddy Ebsen. This was the second Crockett feature strung together from two "World of Disney" episodes. Its popularity led to Fess Parker's long running hit series, "Daniel Boone" (1964–70).

3. THE SIGN OF ZORRO (1960)

D: Norman Foster, Lewis Foster; Guy Williams, Henry Calvin. Not one to leave a good thing unmilked, Disney attempted to repeat his Crocket success with "Zorro" (1957–59). Several episodes were pasted together but the clumsy continuity undermined the charm the series had to offer. The film, however, did well in the foreign market.

4. BATMAN (1966)

D: Leslie Martinson; Adam West, Burt Ward, Burgess Meredith. This was an all-stops-out quickie to cash in on the then-hot dynamic duo's TV series. It was a Bat-flop.

5,6. TARZAN'S DEADLY SILENCE (1970)

D: Robert Friend; Ron Ely, Jock Mahoney, Manuel Padilla
TARZAN'S JUNGLE REBELLION (1970)
D: William Witney; Ron Ely, Manuel Padilla, Sam Jaffe. Both features were multipart episodes of NBC's "Tarzan" (1966–68), and released theatrically as a last-ditch attempt to recoup some of the losses incurred by the extreme difficulties of location filming in Brazil and Mexico.

Fess Parker, as Davy Crockett, and Buddy Ebsen, as Georgie Russell, rode their hugely successful Disney TV miniseries, "Davy Crocket, King of the Wild Frontier," from the miniscreen to the big screen in the first theatrical to be adapted from television series episodes.

7,8. SPIDERMAN (1979)
D: E. W. Swackhamer; Nicholas Hammond
SPIDERMAN STRIKES BACK (1979)
D: Ron Satlof; Nicholas Hammond. Both features were paste-up jobs from the episodes of "The Amazing Spiderman," a series which ran irregularly from its debut in the fall of 1977 through early 1979.

... AND 1 TV MOVIE THAT MADE THE LEAP FROM THE TUBE TO THE SILVER SCREEN

1. BRIAN'S SONG (1970)
D: Buzz Kulik; Billy Dee Williams, James Caan, Jack Warden. A milestone of excellence in the made-for-TV Movies, this film was based on the true story of Brian Piccolo and Gayle Sayers, and their relationship as Chicago Bears football players. The ratings and critical acclaim were so high that the producers released it theatrically, only to learn that movie audiences wouldn't pay to see something they'd seen for nothing on TV. The film's success did, however, catapult relative unknown James Caan into *The Godfather* (1972) and stardom.

3 MOVIES THAT HAVE INSPIRED TV MOVIE SEQUELS

The first thing that happens to a motion picture impregnated by success at the box office is that it's rushed to the delivery room to give birth to a sequel. In the recent past, we've seen *Superman II* (1981); *Oh, God! Book II* (1980); *Smokey and the Bandit II* (1980); *Any Which Way You Can* (1980); *Oliver's Story* (1978); *Jaws II* (1978); *The French Connection II* (1975); *The Godfather II* (1974); to name just a handful, without even mentioning *The Planet of the Apes* and the *Airport* types of series-sequels.

The most recent development in the sequel business has been the TV Movie sequel to a hit motion picture, giving further testimony to the continuously decreasing barriers between the two once-highly competitive mediums.

1. HIGH NOON (1952)
Director: Fred Zinneman; Gary Cooper, Grace Kelly, Lloyd Bridges
HIGH NOON: PART II (CBS), Nov. 15, 1980
Subtitled "The Return of Will Kane," this TV Movie picks up where the classic Western theatrical left off. Only this time around we have Lee Majors in the role that won Cooper an Oscar and Katharine Cannon in the Grace Kelly role. No wonder they call it the *small* screen.

Gary Cooper walked the streets of *High Noon* in 1952, won an Oscar, and inspired Lee Majors to try Cooper's boots on for size in a 1980 TV Movie sequel titled, "High Noon: Part II." And wouldn't you know it? Cooper's boots were much too big for him.

2. THE STEPFORD WIVES (1975)
   D: Bryan Forbes; Katharine Ross, Paula Prentiss, Tina Louise
   THE REVENGE OF THE STEPFORD WIVES (NBC), Oct. 12, 1980
   The continuing saga of the programed, subservient wives featured Sharon
   Gless as a TV reporter who stumbles onto the secret. The only revenge
   that was exacted, however, was on the audience—boredom! Others in
   the cast included Arthur Hill, Julie Kavner, and Mason Adams.
3. ROSEMARY'S BABY (1968)
   D: Roman Polanski; Mia Farrow, John Cassavetes, Ruth Gordon
   LOOK WHAT'S HAPPENED TO ROSEMARY'S BABY (ABC), Nov. 20,
   1978
   Patty Duke Astin, in the Mia Farrow role, is the distraught mother of the
   demon child all grown up—into Stephen McHattie. Only Ruth Gordon
   recreated her movie role as head of a coven of devil worshippers, but not
   even she could breathe life into this uninspired successor to the occult
   classic.

AFTERWORD

I hope that this book was as much fun for you to read as it was for
me to write.

Deadlines and space limitations would not permit us to publish
all of the wonderful, nostalgic trivia and fascinating stuff that we've
unearthed, so, as you might suspect, a second volume, a sort of *Son
of the Book of Movie Lists,* is a distinct possibility.

Any comments you have, corrections, additions, beefs, sugges-
tions for lists, and trivia information, will be gladly received. And if
you're interested in participating in a nationwide poll of All-Time
Movie Favorites, please enclose a self-addressed, stamped envelope
so that we may send you a questionnaire.

Please address all mail to: Gabe Essoe, c/o Arlington House
Publishers, 333 Post Road West, Westport, CT 06880.

Thanks very much.

INDEX